Praying God's Promises Into Suffering

A DEVOTIONAL BIBLE STUDY PRAYER JOURNAL

LAURI A. HOGLE

Copyright © 2023 Singing Christ's Hope
All rights reserved.

No part of this book may be reproduced in any form or by any electronic or mechanical means, including information storage and retrieval systems, without written permission from the author, except for the use of brief quotations in a book review.

Unless otherwise indicated, all Scripture quotations are from The ESV® Bible (The Holy Bible, English Standard Version®), copyright © 2001 by Crossway, a publishing ministry of Good News Publishers. Used by permission. All rights reserved.

Scripture quotations marked CSB have been taken from the Christian Standard Bible®, Copyright © 2017 by Holman Bible Publishers. Used by permission. Christian Standard Bible® and CSB® are federally registered trademarks of Holman Bible Publishers.

Cover photo by Christopher Duden

Trade paperback ISBN: 979-8-9855573-4-3
ePub ISBN: 979-8-9855573-5-0

This book is dedicated to my beloved grandchildren, that they might one day use it on the hard days, the sad days, the days of trial and tribulation.

Nana is praying that, as they pray God's true promises into their suffering, they will find solid hope, comfort, and peace that only comes from trusting in Jesus Christ as Lord and Savior. "Children of the Promise." Nana is praying that God's Word will be His means of ongoing grace to their hurting hearts, as they cling to and pray His promises into every challenge.

♪♪♪

*The Lord has promised good to me.
His Word my hope secures.
He will my shield and portion be,
as long as life endures.*

♪♪♪

Nana loves you, darlings.

Introduction

I woke up at 3 am, writhing in severe pain with a cascade of symptoms within this past year's treatment for my chronic serious illnesses. Stumbling to the kitchen, into my agony, fears, loneliness, and darkness, the coffee cup's Biblical promise made its way through my tears and into my heart.

"The LORD is always with you."

At that moment, God's simple truth calmed me amid my suffering as He reminded me of His Word to me. "Fear not, for I am with you; be not dismayed, for I am your God" (Is. 41:10). "The LORD your God is in your midst...he will quiet you by his love; he will exult over you with loud singing" (Zeph. 3:17).

Messy written pages quickly poured out in the next three hours, with hundreds of Scriptures and unified themes of His Word's promises to me as a follower of Jesus Christ. Songs that echo these promises flooded my mind and soul amid my suffering. Although the symptoms didn't subside, God had soothed my soul, tangibly fulfilling His Zephaniah 3:17 promise. He gave me strengthened endurance in the midst of this fallen world's promised sufferings. I needed solid, sure, and trustworthy promises of truth. I sat in awestruck reverence, knowing I needed to share His encouragement with you. A book had been poured out.

The coffee cup, Scriptures, and songs He'd already tucked away had been God's preparation for this very dark night of my soul. He knew I'd need this practical help, weary in my turmoil and awake with nowhere else to cling. I never planned to write this book, but it has been God's gift of beautiful grace to my heart to write out His promises during this year's journey through my difficult treatment, physically, emotionally, and spiritually.

Even more astounding in God's providential work, several months prior to this book's scheduled publication, He miraculously plopped a renowned neurosurgeon into my life without my seeking one. Similar to what happened in the 90s, we learned I would need another brain surgery as a possible healing treatment for the root cause of my symptoms. This book is God's love gift for that life-changing event.

Beloved in Christ, God's promises are rooted in His unchanging character. They are promises of our loving Abba Father, who is also the Almighty and eternal God. As His promises walk alongside you, notice the verbs! They are usually ongoing and passive; many are His promises regardless of our actions. Notice the source: Father, Son, and Holy Spirit. It is God, our God, Who always keeps His promises.

I'm praying that this devotional prayer journal will help you pray and sing God's promises into your suffering, as a believer in Jesus Christ. I pray that He will enable you to "stand firm in your faith"[1] for another hour, day, month, or year of suffering. If you'd like to dig deeper, enjoy studying and cherishing the promises listed in the notes at the end. For we are indeed standing on the promises of God, as He holds us up by His grace, His gift of ongoing faith in Jesus Christ, into our trials.

Standing on the promises of Christ, my King!
Thro' eternal ages let His praises ring;
"Glory in the highest!" I will shout and sing,
Standing on the promises of God.

Standing on the promises that cannot fail,
When the howling storms of doubt and fear assail,
By the living Word of God I shall prevail,
Standing on the promises of God.

Standing on the promises, I now can see
Perfect, present cleansing in the blood for me;

Standing in the liberty where Christ makes free,
Standing on the promises of God.

Standing on the promises of Christ, the Lord,
Bound to Him eternally by love's strong cord,
Overcoming daily with the Spirit's Sword,
Standing on the promises of God.

Standing on the promises I cannot fall,
List'ning every moment to the Spirit's call,
Resting in my Savior as my All in All,
Standing on the promises of God.

Standing, standing,
Standing on the promises of God, my Savior;
Standing, standing,
I'm standing on the promises of God.

("Standing on the Promises," Cater, R. K., 1886)

God is a promise-keeper

GOD, LONG AGO, YOU MADE A COVENANT PROMISE. FIRST, you told 75-year-old Abram to leave safety and security and move elsewhere. You then promised You'd make a great nation of him and that all the families of this earth would be blessed in him.[1]

As he obeyed You, sometimes his fears took over. He couldn't see how it would be possible. The trip was challenging, with loss and danger. You reminded Abram of Your promise, showing him Your promised land. "Lift up your eyes and look...for all the land..I will give to you and to your offspring forever."[2] He brought his fears and questions to You. Years continued, but he still had no son! How could Your promise come true? You encouraged him, "'Look toward heaven, and number the stars...so shall your offspring be' and he believed."[3] In his trust, You gave him right standing with you.[4] Into his fear, into his waiting, into zero evidence of Your promise fulfilled, You encouraged him as a faithful promise-keeper.

Even though he then tried to take matters into his own hands, not trusting Your timing,[5] You'd already taken responsibility for keeping the whole covenant promise. After 25 years of waiting for fulfillment, You continued to encourage 99-year-old Abram. You renamed him Abraham with Your promises, "I am God Almighty; walk before me, and be blameless, that I may make my covenant between me and you, and may multiply you greatly,"[6] "an everlasting covenant."[7]

Isaac was finally born a year later, with Your upcoming testing of

Abraham's faith. "God will provide for himself the lamb for a burnt offering, my son."[8] You spared Isaac's life after *forty* years of refining Abraham's faith in You, El Shaddai, the promise-keeper. Once again, You promised to bless him, multiplying his offspring into countless numbers. "And your offspring shall possess the gate of his enemies, and in your offspring shall all the nations of the earth be blessed because you have obeyed my voice."[9]

Through the faith You gave him, even when nothing made sense, "no unbelief made him waver concerning the promise of God, but he grew strong in his faith as he gave glory to God, fully convinced that God was able to do what he promised. This is why his faith was counted to him as righteousness."[10] You grew Abraham in all the hard waiting and suffering. You counted him as obedient and in right standing before You, even before giving any commandments to follow. You told him to trust You and keep going, encouraging and giving him the ability to do so.

How does this relate to me as a Christian believer walking through suffering, Lord? Your promise was eternal, to all the families, all the nations. "So then, those who are of faith are blessed along with Abraham, the man of faith."[11] "Now the promises were made to Abraham and to his offspring. It does not say, 'And to offsprings,' referring to many, but referring to one…who is Christ" and "if you are Christ's, then you are Abraham's offspring, heirs according to promise."[12] You are a promise-keeper, fulfilled in Jesus Christ, the Lamb of God You provided…for me.[13]

Through Jesus' perfectly sinless life, death, and resurrection, I am now counted as righteous too, blessed as Your chosen, adopted, redeemed, forgiven, sealed, set apart, accepted, and beloved child.[14] Now and forever, I can lift up my eyes and look to You as my Father because of Jesus, my elder brother in whom Abraham rejoiced. For Jesus, You alone are my righteousness, making me right with God. You are my always-with-me Savior, saying to me as I suffer, "Truly, truly…before Abraham was, 'I am.'"[15]

This is so hard, Lord. I feel...

But You promise...

So I trust You with...

Forgive me for...

Please help me...

My song to you is...

Our God, our help in ages past,
our hope for years to come,
our shelter from the stormy blast,
and our eternal home.

Under the shadow of your throne
your saints have dwelt secure;
sufficient is your arm alone,
and our defense is sure.

Before the hills in order stood,
or earth received her frame,
from everlasting you are God,
to endless years the same.

A thousand ages in your sight
are like an evening gone;
short as the watch that ends the night
before the rising sun.

Our God, our help in ages past,
our hope for years to come:
O be our guard while troubles last,
and our eternal home.

("O God, Our Help in Ages Past," Watts, I., 1719)

♪♪♪

Promises of a faithful God

FAITHFUL GOD, YOU KEPT YOUR COVENANT PROMISE, multiplying Your people and powerfully leading them to Your Promised Land, rescuing them from much turmoil along the way. You saved Your people. Then, in Your faithful and steadfast love, You gave them Your good, righteous, and holy ways to live. Through Moses, You gave Your Law, the Ten Commandments, providing detailed laws of love toward You and one another.

In Your reiterated promised blessings, You began to use the word "if." Your people needed to listen to You and obey Your law. Your promises were conditional on their keeping the covenant.[1]

They failed and failed and failed, deserving not blessings but curses for their disobedience.[2] Yet, You continually gave them opportunities to turn back to You in wholehearted obedience, with total forgiveness. Your promises, held in "if-then" statements, became inward, "so that you will love the LORD your God with all your heart and with all your soul, that you may live."[3] "Therefore, choose life...loving the LORD your God obeying his voice and holding fast to him."[4]

Lord, You already knew they would turn away from You and Your Old Covenant law of love, bringing evil living, suffering, and death along with it.[5] Yet, You kept Your covenant promise, no matter how much they rebelled: "I will never leave you nor forsake you."[6]

Your word is not conditional here.

It is "never."

"I have loved you with an everlasting love; therefore I have continued my faithfulness to you" (Jer. 31:3).

Although Your people couldn't obey Your Law because they walked in their inborn sin, Your "never" highlights Your faithful promise... because You already had a plan, created from all eternity.

"She will bear a son, and you shall call his name Jesus, for he will save his people from their sins. All this took place to fulfill what the Lord had spoken by the prophet: 'Behold, the virgin shall conceive and bear a son, and they shall call his name, Immanuel' (which means, God with us)."[7]

Fully human and fully God, Jesus came to earth to live a perfectly sinless and obedient life, satisfying all of Your "if-then" requirements.[8] No one else can ever possibly keep Your law perfectly because "none is righteous, no, not one...no one is good, not even one."[9] We simply can't, as sinners.

But as our faithful promise-keeper, Jesus "humbled himself by becoming obedient to the point of death, even death on a cross."[10] Jesus paid the full penalty of death, required by the Law, so that those who trust in Him for salvation will never have to. It was through His blood, not the blood of the many animals offered as needed sacrifices when Your people broke the law. By His blood, You have entirely and faithfully secured eternal life with You forever,[11] because You are a faithful promise-keeper.

"For the law was given through Moses; grace and truth came through Jesus Christ" (Jn. 1:17).

As I suffer, I sing today along with all my brothers and sisters in Christ who also suffered in their earthly lives, and are now enjoying the blessings of Your faithful promises to us! "Blessed be the God and Father of our Lord Jesus Christ, who has blessed us in Christ with every spiritual blessing in the heavenly places, even as he chose us in him before the foundation of the world that we should be holy and blameless before him."[12]

This is so hard, Lord. I feel...

But You promise...

So I trust You with...

Forgive me for...

Please help me...

My song to you is...

Great is thy faithfulness, O God my Father;
there is no shadow of turning with thee;
thou changest not, thy compassions, they fail not;
as thou hast been thou forever wilt be.

Great is thy faithfulness!
Great is thy faithfulness!
Morning by morning new mercies I see:
all I have needed thy hand hath provided -
Great is thy faithfulness, Lord, unto me!

Summer and winter and springtime and harvest,
sun, moon, and stars in their courses above,
join with all nature in manifold witness
to thy great faithfulness, mercy, and love.

Pardon for sin and a peace that endureth,
thine own dear presence to cheer and to guide,
strength for today and bright hope for tomorrow,
blessings all mine, with ten thousand beside!

("Great is Thy Faithfulness," Chisholm, T. O., 1923)

♪♪♪

God's amazing "New Covenant" promises!

FATHER, WITHIN YOUR GLORIOUS LOVE STORY TO YOUR people, Your eternal covenant promises are now fulfilled in Jesus Christ, through the "new covenant" in His blood.[1] You gave these promises throughout the Old Testament, and You've fulfilled so many of them already.[2] By Your Spirit's work,[3] I now treasure Your promise of the gospel. You've made the Old Covenant obsolete through the sinless obedience of Jesus, His atoning death in my place, and His victorious resurrection.[4] As I read Your words of the Old Covenant, please remind me of what is now true for me as one who has been redeemed.

"Christ redeemed us from the curse of the law by becoming a curse for us...so that in Christ Jesus the blessing of Abraham might come to the Gentiles, so that we might receive the promised Spirit through faith" (Gal. 3:13-14).

"For Christ also suffered for sins once for all, the righteous for the unrighteous, that he might bring you to God. He was put to death in the flesh but made alive by the Spirit" (1 Pet. 3:18 CSB).

"Everyone who lives and believes in me will never die" (Jn. 11:25 CSB).

Now, You've graciously given me so many promises as one who trusts in You for salvation, for I do believe! This is my obedience, having turned to You in repentance and belief, Lord Jesus. No matter what earthly suffering I endure in my earthly life, Your promises are true.

"***I will*** put my laws into their minds, and write them on their hearts, and ***I will*** be their God, and they ***shall*** be my people" (Heb. 8:10 emphasis added).

"I, I am he who blots out your transgressions for my own sake, and I will not remember your sins" (Is. 43:25).

Suffering is such a tempting time to doubt Your gospel promises, Lord. But, into my tears and fears, help me remember that it's by Your gracious gift of faith that I even *can* trust You; it's not anything in myself. For I needed to be crucified with Christ, with my inborn sin nature nailed to the cross; now, it's not my old self that is alive, but You are living in me by Your indwelling Holy Spirit.[5] I am Your new creation *in* Christ![6] It's in my union *with* Jesus Christ that I can trust Your promises and plans, for Your promises are only "yes" in Jesus.[7]

So, my promise-keeping God of covenant love, as I read and sing of all of Your precious promises to me, guard my emotions and thoughts. Help me to remember that I only have Your promises in Christ, through Christ, because of Christ, and with Christ, my beloved risen and reigning Savior who prays for me:

"Father, I desire that they also whom you have given me, may be with me where I am, to see my glory that you have given me because you loved me before the foundation of the world" (Jn. 17:24).

To the praise of His glory and Your glorious grace to me!

This is so hard, Lord. I feel...

But You promise...

So I trust You with...

Forgive me for...

Please help me...

My song to you is...

Abide with me: fast falls the eventide;
the darkness deepens; Lord, with me abide:
when other helpers fail, and comforts flee,
help of the helpless, O abide with me.

Swift to its close ebbs out life's little day;
earth's joys grow dim, its glories pass away;
change and decay in all around I see;
O thou who changest not, abide with me.

I need thy presence ev'ry passing hour;
what but thy grace can foil the tempter's pow'r?
Who like thyself my guide and stay can be?
Through cloud and sunshine, O abide with me.

I fear no foe, with thee at hand to bless;
ills have no weight, and tears no bitterness.
Where is death's sting? Where, grave, thy victory?
I triumph still, if thou abide with me.

Hold thou thy cross before my closing eyes;
shine through the gloom, and point me to the skies:
heav'n's morning breaks, and earth's vain shadows flee:
in life, in death, O Lord, abide with me.

("Abide with Me," Lyte, H. F., 1847)

♪♪♪

Amazing grace, how sweet the sound

FATHER, AS I SUFFER, PLEASE HELP ME TO SING THE PROMISES of Your amazing grace, for the sound is very sweet. Remind me continually that I suffer differently than those who do not know Jesus as Lord and Savior. For I suffer, but as Your rescued, beloved child. I suffer now, but my eternal inheritance is secure as a believer in Christ![1]

With the riches of Your grace lavished on me by giving me faith in Christ, I already have redemption and forgiveness for every sin, and I've been made right with You, apart from my own works.[2]

As one of those You've graciously called to Yourself, You're now conforming me to the image of Jesus as I walk this earth. As I suffer. Oh, how my beloved Jesus suffered as He lived on earth...all for me. So I know You're working all things together for good, always for me as my always-loving God and Father.[3]

I'm waiting for Jesus now, in this time of redemption. You promise so much when He returns! I long and yearn for Your promised future day when You make all things new,[4] the day when I will see Him as He is,[5] the day when You restore all things to Your perfect creation.[6] But You aren't yet finished with bringing Your sheep to Yourself. By Your grace, You are right now saving Your people, transferring them from the domain of darkness into the kingdom of Jesus Christ.[7] And when Jesus returns to judge every human being, He's going to save those who eagerly look forward to being with Him forever![8] It's all Your promise!

So, help me to sing of Your amazing grace toward me as I suffer today. Remind me that it's never been my own goodness, righteous acts, or anything of myself that earns this life with You. I am in Christ only because of Your gift of grace and trusting faith, all because of what Jesus has done for me. So I can rest in Your promises.

"For by grace you **have been** saved through faith. And this is not your own doing; it is the gift of God, not a result of works, so that no one may boast" (Eph. 2:8, emphasis added).

"The one who believes in the Son **has** eternal life, but the one who rejects the Son will not see life; instead, the wrath of God remains on him" (Jn. 3:36 CSB, emphasis added).

"If you confess with your mouth that Jesus is Lord and believe in your heart that God raised him from the dead, you **will be saved**" (Rom. 10:9, emphasis added).

"The LORD waits to be gracious to you…He will surely be gracious to you at the sound of your cry. As soon as he hears it, he answers you" (Is. 30:18, 19).

"Everyone who believes in [Jesus] receives forgiveness of sins through his name" (Acts 10:43).

"For all have sinned and fall short of the glory of God, and are justified by his grace as a gift, through the redemption that is in Christ Jesus" (Rom. 3:23-24).

Fill me with gratitude and awe of Your grace, Father. Help me to share Your promised grace found in the gospel of Jesus Christ with those who don't believe "there is salvation in no one else."[9] Help me to remember that I suffer, but within this appointed historical time of Your redemption, one in which You are opening eyes "so that they may turn from darkness to light, and from the power of Satan to God, that they may receive forgiveness of sins and a place among those who are sanctified by faith in (Jesus)."[10]

Stir me, Lord, away from any self-righteous pride or fear and toward deepened love for You and others in new and special ways. Could this be part of Your call to me today, precisely because I'm suffering?

"And God is able to make **all** grace abound to you, so that having **all** sufficiency, in **all** things, at **all** times, you may abound in every good work" (2 Cor. 9:8, emphasis added).

"And after you have suffered a little while, the God of all grace, who has called you to his eternal glory in Christ, **will himself** restore, confirm, strengthen, and establish you" (1 Pet. 5:10, emphasis added).

This is so hard, Lord. I feel...

But You promise...

So I trust You with...

Forgive me for...

Please help me...

My song to you is...

Amazing grace! -- how sweet the sound--
that saved a wretch like me!
I once was lost, but now am found,
was blind, but now I see.

'Twas grace that taught my heart to fear,
and grace my fears relieved;
how precious did that grace appear
the hour I first believed!

Thro' many dangers, toils, and snares,
I have already come;
'tis grace has brought me safe thus far,
and grace will lead me home.

The Lord has promised good to me,
his Word my hope secures;
he will my shield and portion be,
as long as life endures.

And when this flesh and heart shall fail,
and mortal life shall cease,
I shall possess within the veil
a life of joy and peace.

When we've been there ten thousand years,
bright shining as the sun,
we've no less days to sing God's praise
than when we've first begun.

("Amazing Grace," Newton, J., 1779)

♪♪♪

Our Promised Land

FATHER, YOU CONTINUALLY REMINDED YOUR PEOPLE OF what they would experience in Your promised land. It kept them going in the harsh, winding, exhausting, painful journey that lasted an entire generation.[1] Now, Your promises carry me in my suffering journey. For their promised land was only a foreshadowing of my own future home.

"According to his promise we are waiting for new heavens and a new earth in which righteousness dwells" (2 Pet. 3:13).

Jesus Himself is my only righteousness![2] He is alive, victoriously living right now in a resurrected body, seated at Your right hand![3] Because You called and raised me to new life with Him already,[4] You promise that I will always live with Him in this land, with a transformed and glorious resurrected body like His.[5] I will live in the perfect place Jesus has already prepared for me[6] in my "New Covenant" eternal inheritance![7]

What a tremendous promise that sustains me on the most challenging days. I read of Your promised land and can't imagine its sinless, perfectly restored beauty. I can't wait for the endless feasts,[8] the wedding feast as I join with all of the bride of Christ You created in this current time of redemption,[9] within the sinless safety of all You've transformed,[10] seeing the brilliant sights of Revelation 21 and 22.

But most of all, I can't wait to live with You.

Your covenant promises will be fulfilled entirely, for all of eternity.

"For the Lamb in the midst of the throne will be their shepherd, and he will guide them to springs of living water, and God will wipe away every tear from their eyes" (Rev. 7:17).

As I suffer in this decaying body and fallen world infected by sin and all of the resulting sufferings, please fill me with constant hope as I imagine and look forward to Your eternal promise.[11] In the most harrowing moments, help me to remember that Your unchanging goodness and compassionate mercy follow me every single day of this earthly suffering and that You promise I *will* live with You in Your house, forever.[12]

On the hardest days, help me to sing of Your glory, as a foreshadowing of what is to come. When I see glimpses of Your glory in Your creation,[13] or re-turn to Your glory in Jesus Christ,[14] and enjoy Your glorious gifts of feasting and loved ones,[15] point my heart to praising You, my glorious Promise-keeper.

For You promise that I will one day join in the unending song of praise to You!

"Holy, holy, holy is the LORD of hosts; the whole earth is full of his glory!" (Is. 6:3)

"Worthy is the Lamb who was slain, to receive power and wealth and wisdom and might and honor and glory and blessing!" (Rev. 5:12)

This is so hard, Lord. I feel...

But You promise...

So I trust You with...

Forgive me for...

Please help me...

My song to you is...

O Christ, our hope, our heart's desire,
redemption's only spring!
Creator of the world art thou,
its Savior and its King.

How vast the mercy and the love
which laid our sins on thee,
and led thee to a cruel death,
to set thy people free.

But now the bands of death are burst,
the ransom has been paid;
and thou art on thy Father's throne,
in glorious robes arrayed.

O Christ, be thou our lasting joy,
our ever great reward!
Our only glory may it be
to glory in the Lord.

("O Christ, Our Hope, Our Heart's Desire," Chandler, J., 1837)

♪♪♪

God promises His abiding presence and fruit

Father, You encouraged Your people to be strong, without fear or dread, before they ventured into already-known hardship. How?

"For it is the LORD your God who goes with you. He will not leave you or forsake you" (Deut. 31:8).

Your promise came true, of course.[1] As I face sure suffering in this world, You continue to promise Your abiding presence, an already-true reality.

"For I will pour water on the thirsty land, and streams on the dry ground; I will pour my Spirit upon your offspring, and my blessing on your descendants" (Is. 44:3).

The offspring You were describing? It's Jesus. He is my poured-out blessing as I suffer,[2] my living water,[3] whose blood of the New Covenant was poured out for me.[4]

"Whoever drinks of the water that I will give him will never be thirsty again. The water that I will give him will become in him a spring of water welling up to everlasting life" (Jn. 4:14).

Jesus promised to send the Holy Spirit as my Helper,[5] which came true in Acts 2. So now, You've established, anointed, and sealed me and every true believer with the gift of Your indwelling Spirit.[6] As Your beloved child, He is within me, every moment of this suffering, as the guarantee of my heavenly inheritance.[7]

Holy Spirit, You promise to give me godly new desires,[8] to cause me to walk in obedience[9] as You continually and progressively sanctify and set me apart in holiness.[10] You promise that I "will not gratify the desires of the flesh" as You empower me to "walk by the Spirit."[11] How? You are interceding for me according to God's will, helping me in my human weakness.[12] You're illuminating Your living and active Word and its truth to my heart,[13] growing, protecting, teaching, counseling, and leading me.[14]

> "And we all, with unveiled face, beholding the glory of the Lord, are being transformed into the same image from one degree of glory to another. For this comes from the Lord who is the Spirit" (2 Cor. 3:18)!

Lord, this is all Your promised work! You promise that "He who is in you is greater than he who is in the world."[15] When my suffering squeezes and sin threatens, I'm clinging to Your promises, all enabled by Your Holy Spirit abiding in me and transforming me...in and through this suffering time of fruit-bearing growth.

For You promise that I will bear Your Galatians 5 fruit, even amid my suffering or sinful failures. You promise to grow love, joy, and peace within me. You promise to cultivate patience, kindness, and goodness in me as I interact with others. You promise to develop faithfulness, gentleness, and self-control as I walk through earthly trials, producing a "harvest of righteousness."[16] You will fill me with the "fruit of righteousness that comes through Jesus Christ, to the glory and praise of God."[17]

> "Now may the God of peace himself sanctify you completely, and may your whole spirit and soul and body be kept blameless at the coming of our Lord Jesus Christ.
>
> He who calls you is faithful; **he will surely do it**" (1 Thess. 5:23-24, emphasis added).

This is so hard, Lord. I feel...

But You promise...

So I trust You with...

Forgive me for...

Please help me...

My song to you is...

Spirit of God, dwell thou within my heart;
wean it from earth, through all its pulses move;
stoop to my weakness, mighty as thou art,
and make me love thee as I ought to love.

I ask no dream, no prophet ecstasies,
no sudden rending of the veil of clay,
no angel visitant, no opening skies;
but take the dimness of my soul away.

Hast thou not bid us love thee, God and King?
All, all thine own, soul, heart, and strength and mind.
I see thy cross--there teach my heart to cling:
O let me seek thee, and O let me find.

Teach me to feel that thou art always nigh;
teach me the struggles of the soul to bear,
to check the rising doubt, the rebel sigh;
teach me the patience of unanswered prayer.

Teach me to love thee as thine angels love,
one holy passion filling all my frame;
the baptism of the heaven-descended Dove,
my heart an altar, and thy love the flame.

("Spirit of God, Descend Upon my Heart," Croly, G., 1854)

♪♪♪

God's promise of peace

Father, because I have been justified by faith in the Lord Jesus Christ, the Prince of Peace,[1] I have peace with You now and forever.[2] This peace with You is a wholeness of belonging to You, a settled well-being, no matter what my earthly circumstances hold. I praise You for Your covenant promise of peace to me as Your believing child. For Jesus himself is my peace, reconciling me to You, through His death on the cross in my place.[3] This is the "gospel of peace" that helps me stand strong in evil and dark days.[4]

> "'For the mountains may depart and the hills be removed, but my steadfast love shall not depart from you, and my covenant of peace shall not be removed,' says the LORD, who has compassion on you" (Is. 54:10).

No wonder the multitude, maybe thousands, of angels filled the sky with Your praise as Jesus was born! "Glory to God in the highest, and on earth peace among those with whom he is pleased!"[5]

Yet, in moments when it feels like the world is crumbling and my mind swirls to possible scary future events, I also desperately need to feel the calm and tranquil peace that You promise me as a believer in Christ. Because You promise suffering and tribulation in this world, I need the things You've said in Your Word to have this peace.[6] For You often connect peace with times of suffering, included in "all things" we experience on earth. You describe peace as Your gift "at *all* times in *every* way."[7]

You promise to give me peace that protects my emotions and thoughts as I suffer,[8] with blossomed contentment in my suffering,[9] knowing that You will supply all I need to endure earthly suffering, just as You did with Jesus.[10]

This peace, one that surpasses human or worldly understanding, comes from Your indwelling Holy Spirit.[11] So Lord, please help me to set my mind on Him,[12] as He teaches and reminds me of Your Word.[13] You tell me to "let the peace of Christ rule" in my emotions and heart by letting "the word of Christ dwell" in me richly. Singing, rejoicing always, and being thankful to You are all part of this process![14]

It's Your promise, all the way to the end of Your love story of perfect peace! "You keep him in perfect peace whose mind is stayed on you, because he trusts in you."[15] "O LORD, you will ordain peace for us, for you have indeed done for us all our works."[16]

I want to be supernaturally free from fears or anxiety as suffering multiplies. I want Jesus to find me "at peace" on Your promised day of judgment.[17] As I pray for so much and so many, help me to sink into Your Word's promises, satisfied and content with what You're doing right now and trusting You for what is to come. Stay and settle my mind with complete trust, Lord!

"In peace I will both lie down and sleep; for you alone, O LORD, make me dwell in safety" (Ps. 4:8).

"I awake, and I am still with you" (Ps. 139:18).

This is so hard, Lord. I feel...

But You promise...

So I trust You with...

Forgive me for...

Please help me...

My song to you is...

Like a river glorious is God's perfect peace,
over all victorious in its bright increase;
perfect, yet it floweth fuller ev'ry day,
perfect, yet it groweth deeper all the way.

Stayed upon Jehovah, hearts are fully blest,
finding, as he promised, perfect peace and rest.

Hidden in the hollow of his blessed hand,
never foe can follow, never traitor stand;
not a surge of worry, not a shade of care,
not a blast of hurry, touch the spirit there.

Stayed upon Jehovah, hearts are fully blest,
finding, as he promised, perfect peace and rest.

Ev'ry joy or trial falleth from above,
traced upon our dial by the Sun of Love.
We may trust him fully all for us to do;
they who trust him wholly find him wholly true.

Stayed upon Jehovah, hearts are fully blest,
finding, as he promised, perfect peace and rest.

("Like a River Glorious," Havergal, F. R., 1874)

♪♪♪

God's promise of love

My loving Father, this is perhaps Your most tremendous promise to me as Your child of covenant and everlasting love.

> "Neither death nor life, nor angels nor rulers, nor things present nor things to come, nor powers, nor height nor depth, nor anything else in all creation, will be able to separate us from the love of God in Christ Jesus our Lord" (Rom. 8:38-39).

Oh God Who *is* love,[1] You've proven Your love in Jesus' death for me, taking my just penalty for the inborn sin that separated me from You and clothing me in Your righteousness instead.[2] I love You only because You first loved me![3] Because I trust in Jesus for salvation, I now can look forward to eternal life with You.[4] With this promise, help me live in today's suffering with a deepened awareness of Your steadfast love for me, today.[5]

> "Who shall separate us from the love of Christ? Shall tribulation, or distress, or persecution, or famine, or nakedness, or danger, or sword?" (Rom. 8:36).

Help me to rest in the truth of Your perfect love for me, never fearing You're punishing me with suffering.[6] Protect my heart and thoughts, armoring up in Your promised love, shown to me in the salvation You've given to me in Christ. Because, if nothing at all can separate me from Your love, this means I am living together with Jesus right now, in today's suffering.[7]

It's all *through* Jesus, because *of* Jesus, by the person and work of Jesus *for* me! I am together *with* Jesus and *in* Jesus!

What a promise! Trusting Your love-promise of living with my beloved Jesus now...as I suffer with the hard-normal trials that happen to everyone in this fallen world? This is Your promised victory for those in Christ! For it's the fruit of Your indwelling Holy Spirit that I can rest in Your love for me.

> "God's love has been poured into our hearts through the Holy Spirit who has been given to us" (Rom. 5:5).

My loving Father, in this brutal battle of suffering, remind me every morning of Your steadfast love for me in Christ.[8] Fill me with Your Spirit, so I intimately *know* this love that takes me beyond intellectual belief, into heart dwelling.[9] Give me strong roots as You ground me in Your unchanging character of love.[10]

For You tell me to love You with all my heart, soul, mind, and strength,[11] believing in the character or name of Your Son, Jesus Christ, and loving others.[12] So, my most profound need is to completely trust in Your promised love as I suffer. Jesus promises me, along with all of Your believing children, "I have made known to them your name, and I will continue to make it known, that the love with which you have loved me may be in them, and I in them."[13]

From this beloved place,[14] through Your Spirit's continual reminders of Your gospel gift of promised love fulfilled in Christ, I can then love You and others as myself,[15] even as I suffer. Maybe I could pray for them or share Your promised love with them today. Show me, loving God.

> "As the Father has loved me, so have I loved you. Abide in my love" (John 15:9).

> "But this I call to mind, and therefore I have hope: The steadfast love of the LORD never ceases" (Lam. 3:21-22).

This is so hard, Lord. I feel...

But You promise...

So I trust You with...

Forgive me for...

Please help me...

My song to you is...

O Love that wilt not let me go,
I rest my weary soul in thee;
I give thee back the life I owe,
that in thine ocean depths its flow
may richer, fuller be.

O Light that follow'st all my way,
I yield my flick'ring torch to thee;
my heart restores its borrowed ray,
that in thy sunshine's blaze its day
may brighter, fairer be.

O Joy that seekest me through pain
I cannot close my heart to thee;
I trace the rainbow through the rain,
and feel the promise is not vain
that morn shall tearless be.

O Cross that liftest up my head,
I dare not ask to fly from thee;
I lay in dust life's glory dead,
and from the ground there blossoms red
life that shall endless be.

("O Love, That Wilt Not Let Me Go," Matheson, G., 1882)

♪♪♪

God's promise of joy

Father, Jesus says that His joy is completed in me through the words He's spoken and that my joy is in Him because He is in me.¹ What is Your promised joy? Is it an emotion of happiness? Sometimes, but the original Greek for "joy" also means "calm delight." Calm delight is Your promised fruit of the Holy Spirit. I hunger for this fruit today. My Helper, please help me to walk by You today, growing Your "calm delight" into me.² Please remind me of Your promised gift of joy, into this suffering time.

You tell me to rejoice, always.³ Of course, "always" includes my earthly suffering. But I can't create or muster up joy when my emotions are all over the place. Maybe Your gift of joy is one I need to simply receive. Perhaps it's mine to "take."

> "Though the fig tree does not blossom, nor fruit be on the vines...yet I will **take joy** in the God of my salvation (Hab. 3:17-18, emphasis added).

Maybe I need to ask You for Your promised joy, to reach for Your joy and hold onto it. Perhaps my joy could be found wholly in Your gift of salvation, as You again help me remember Your gospel promise.

> "With joy you **will** draw water from the wells of salvation" (Is. 12:3, emphasis added).

For this promise was one I simply "took" and received as Your gift of grace to me on the day You opened my eyes, turned me away from the power of Satan and darkness, brought me to Yourself and Your light, forgave my sins, and gave me a place in Your kingdom by faith in Christ.[4] Maybe Your gift of joy is stirred when I remember Your amazing love for me, in doing all of this in and for me.

Maybe my joy is in resting in my union with Jesus now, calmly delighting in Your promised reunion with Jesus one glorious and joy-full day.[5] For through Him, I can rejoice that You've already given me the gift of "reconciliation" with You.[6] Could this precious and promised gift of Your calm delight be something that carries me in this suffering, regardless of my many swirling emotions?

Oh glorious and mighty God, please strengthen me to endure this suffering patiently and with Your joy.[7] I remember the joy when You saved me...restore this same joy to me today, as You hold me up "with a willing spirit."[8] God of hope, by Your Spirit's power, fill me with all joy that comes from believing the gospel once again today.[9] For this is all Your promised work in my heart. It relies on You, so I look to You for the fulfillment of Your promise.

Jesus, it was "for the joy that was set before" You that You endured all the suffering of the cross, the suffering I deserved.[10] My being saved was Your joy as You suffered. My own calm delight, completing Your joy, comes from trusting the gifts of Your Word's promises, fulfilled in Your perfect timing and will and according to Your unchanging character and name. So, as You promised Your disciples, help me to keep going, with Your calm delight:

"You have sorrow now, but I will see you again, and your hearts will rejoice, and no one will take your joy from you" (Jn. 16:22).

"Until now you have asked nothing in my name. Ask, and you will receive, that your joy may be full" (Jn. 16:24).

"Now to him who is able to do far more abundantly than all we ask or think, according to the power at work ***within*** us, to him be glory in the church and in Christ Jesus throughout all generations, forever and ever. Amen" (Eph. 3:20-21, emphasis added).

This is so hard, Lord. I feel...

But You promise...

So I trust You with...

Forgive me for...

Please help me...

My song to you is...

I've found the pearl of greatest price!
My heart doth sing for joy;
and sing I must, for Christ is mine!
Christ shall my song employ.

Christ is my Prophet, Priest, and King;
My Prophet full of light,
my great High Priest before the throne,
my King of heav'nly might.

For he indeed is Lord of lords,
and he the King of kings;
he is the Sun of Righteousness,
with healing in his wings.

Christ is my peace; he died for me,
for me he shed his blood;
and as my wondrous sacrifice,
offered himself to God.

Christ Jesus is my all in all,
my comfort and my love;
my life below, and he shall be
my joy and crown above.

("I've Found the Pearl of Greatest Price!" by J. Mason, 1683)

♪♪♪

God's promise of patience

My patient Father, I'm coming to You today as I ponder the beautiful Hebrew word for patient..."longsuffering."

My suffering feels so long right now. So, please grant me Your longsuffering patience into my natural impatience with this continual challenge. Along with all of Your perfect creation directly affected by the fall into sin, I "groan inwardly" as I wait.[1] Amid continual trouble, please help me to be patient as Galatians 5 fruit of Your indwelling Spirit, patient as "longsuffering."

I praise You that You are "slow to anger."[2] This definition of "patient" is so humbling when I re-realize how much I deserve Your anger for my sin against You. But You are "a God merciful and gracious, slow to anger, and abounding in steadfast love and faithfulness."[3]

You're so patient with me that You gave Jesus for me. You gave me to Jesus. Not only are You slow to anger, but You've removed Your righteous wrath for sin, for those in Christ.[4] My suffering is not Your anger toward me! You've completely lifted this from me in Your great patience and overwhelming love and grace. I am now Your beloved in Christ! Oh, Father, thank You!

Maybe Your loving gospel gift will help me continually re-turn to Jesus in my impatience. For it's in the hard waiting as I suffer that You promise to give me patience.

You promise to strengthen me with Your power, according to Your "glorious might," for "all endurance and patience with joy."[5]

Patience to endure suffering is a gift that comes from You, glorious and mighty Lord! And my need for patience turns me to You, for I'm actually waiting patiently *for* You.[6] I'm excitedly waiting for the adoption and redemption of my body, with a sure hope in what I can't see, the eternal things.[7] As I "longsuffer," I'm longing for my true home, for I'm now a citizen of heaven.[8] I'm often impatiently waiting for Jesus to return while knowing that You aren't slow in fulfilling Your glorious promise in the way I would consider time. No, You're waiting for each of Your children to "reach repentance."[9]

"Rejoice in hope, be patient in tribulation, be constant in prayer" (Rom. 12:12).

Please help me cling to Your promises so that I can patiently endure this suffering, by Your Spirit's work through Your Word. Establish my heart with patience as I wait for the coming of my glorious Lord Jesus with hope.[10] As Your chosen one, holy and beloved, help me to put on patience.[11] Help me to be still before You and wait patiently for You.[12]

I cling to Your promise as I wait:

"The LORD will fulfill his purpose for me" (Ps. 138:8).

You continually remind me that Your promised plan and purpose is to conform me to the image of Your beloved Son, my beloved Savior.[13] Jesus Christ displayed His "perfect patience" as an example to me.[14] So, by Your grace, I too can be patient for Your fulfilled promises as You fill me with Your Spirit, with Your resulting, promised fruit of "longsuffering" patience. "For God alone my soul waits in silence; from him comes my salvation."[15] "I wait for the LORD, my soul wait, and in his word I hope."[16]

"The one who endures to the end **will be** saved" (Mt. 24:13, emphasis added).

This is so hard, Lord. I feel...

But You promise...

So I trust You with...

Forgive me for...

Please help me...

My song to you is...

Spirit of God, descend upon my heart;
wean it from earth, through all its pulses move;
stoop to my weakness, mighty as thou art,
and make me love thee as I ought to love.

I ask no dream, no prophet ecstasies,
no sudden rending of the veil of clay,
no angel visitant, no op'ning skies;
but take the dimness of my soul away.

Hast thou not bid us love thee, God and King?
All, all thine own, soul, heart, and strength and mind.
I see the cross– there teach my heart to cling:
O let me seek thee, and O let me find.

Teach me to feel that thou art always nigh;
teach me the struggles of the soul to bear,
to check the rising doubt, the rebel sigh;
teach me the patience of unanswered prayer.

Teach me to love thee as thine angels love,
one holy passion filling all my frame:
the baptism of the heav'n-descended Dove,
my heart an altar, and thy love the flame.

("Spirit of God, Descend Upon my Heart," Croly, G., 1854)

♪♪♪

God's promise of kindness

Father, the fruit of Your Holy Spirit includes kindness. This is a facet of Your unchanging character that we often forget when suffering. But Your kindness, in all of its riches, is Your gift that leads us to repentance as we turn to You and away from our sin.[1] You describe this as leading us "with cords of kindness, with the bands of love," easing our yoke, bending down to us and feeding us.[2]

Jesus echoes Your kindness when He reminds me to take His easy yoke and light burden upon myself, to learn from Him, my gentle and lowly Savior, finding rest for my soul.[3] He promises, "I will give you rest."[4] As I suffer, help me to stay yoked with Jesus as I remember Your kind promises to me.

Because You've already saved me, raising me and seating me with Christ, You promise "that in the coming ages" You will "show the immeasurable riches" of Your "kindness toward" me "in Christ Jesus."[5] This is because Your saving me was entirely Your gift of grace to me, in Your love and kindness toward me.

"He saved us, not because of works done by us in righteousness, but according to his own mercy, by the washing of regeneration and renewal of the Holy Spirit, whom he poured out on us richly through Jesus Christ our Savior, so that being justified by his grace we might become heirs according to the hope of eternal life" (Titus 3:5-7).

Lord, in today's suffering, I can rest in Your kindness. For You are kind in all of Your works.[6] I feel like I'm enduring overwhelming troubles and I'm so tempted to think I have it worse than others. I read of Paul's "afflictions, hardships, calamities, beatings, imprisonments, riots, labors, sleepless nights, hungers,"[7] and I'm humbled by Your kindness in leaving me Your Word and so many promises in these very contexts.

I read of my beloved Savior and what He endured on the cross for me and I'm humbled by Your kindness to me in sparing me from deserved punishment for my sin, a suffering far worse than any believer has or will experience. Jesus lived through this separation from You while bearing the complete weight of sin.

Oh Father, You now continue to turn me to You, leading and feeding me in Your kindness. It is ongoing and unchanging. You promise to grow me, as I suffer, by the work of Your Holy Spirit. You promise to help me "keep in step with the Spirit"[8] so that I can be kind and tenderhearted, forgiving others.[9] You promise to shape me into a Proverbs 31 kind of woman who speaks "the teaching of kindness."[10]

What a fantastic promise, Lord! Your yoke is indeed easy! You are leading me by Your Spirit, in Your kindness, carrying and bearing me up as I walk yoked with Jesus, my Lord and Savior. When I heard the gospel of my salvation and trusted Him, You sealed me with Your "promised Holy Spirit who is the guarantee of our inheritance until we acquire possession of it, to the praise of his glory."[11]

So by Your Spirit, You promise to work in me to want to obey You, to walk yoked with Jesus, and to "work for his good pleasure."[12] In Your immense kindness of drawing, saving, leading, and holding me up, You promise:

> "He who began a good work in you **will** bring it to completion at the day of Jesus Christ" (Phil. 1:6, emphasis added).

This is so hard, Lord. I feel...

But You promise...

So I trust You with...

Forgive me for...

Please help me...

My song to you is...

*In loving-kindness Jesus came
my soul in mercy to reclaim,
and from the depths of sin and shame
thro' grace he lifted me.*

*From sinking sand he lifted me,
with tender hand he lifted me,
from shades of night to plains of light,
oh, praise his name, he lifted me!*

*He called me long before I heard,
before my sinful heart was stirred,
but when I took him at his word,
forgiv'n he lifted me.*

*His brow was pierced with many a thorn,
his hands by cruel nails were torn,
when from my guilt and grief, forlorn,
in love he lifted me.*

*Now on a higher plane I dwell,
and with my soul I know 'tis well;
yet how or why, I cannot tell,
he should have lifted me*

("He Lifted Me," Gabriel, C. H., 1905)

♪♪♪

God's promise of goodness

Father, yesterday's sweet Philippians 1:6 promise of goodness mingles with Your mercy and compassion toward me as one of Your sheep. As with all Your promises, it derives from Your unchanging goodness. Your goodness is sure; it is trustworthy.

"Surely goodness and mercy shall follow me all the days of my life, and I shall dwell in the house of the LORD forever" (Ps. 23:6).

All the days of my life. That includes today, a day of earthly suffering.

So, today I cling to Your sure promise of goodness. You promise that for those who love You and are called according to Your perfect plan and purpose, "all things work together for good."[1] I'm reminded of Joseph, who endured years of suffering at his brothers' hands. Yet, though they "meant evil" for him, You "meant it for good."[2] And what was the greatest good that came from it all? You physically protected and sustained the tribe of Judah, fulfilling Your covenant promise. Through all of the horrific in Joseph's life, You fulfilled Your redemptive plan and promise in bringing Your Son to earth. And now, You've drawn me to Jesus Christ in Your goodness and mercy toward me. These events of Your glorious love story were so much bigger than what Joseph could see.

Please help me to taste and see[3] Your promised goodness, Father of lights, for You are indeed unchanging in Your goodness and Your good and perfect gifts to me.[4] Somehow, this hard day is included. In Your infinite wisdom and good plan for my life, You promise to give good things who ask, seek, and knock.[5]

This suffering is undoubtedly increasing my soul's longing, thirst, and hunger for You, in deepened dependence on You for so many needs. Could my need for Your continual help be a good thing that You've promised to me as Your beloved daughter?

"For he satisfies the longing soul, and the hungry soul he fills with good things" (Ps. 107:9).

"The LORD is good, a stronghold in a day of distress; he cares for those who take refuge in him" (Nah. 1:7 CSB).

Could it be that You're carrying and leading me, Good Shepherd,[6] as I walk through the darkest valley? For You promise that, in the good work You're doing in me, You will help me fight doubts and fears so I can trust You[7] until the day I finally see You.

For because of Your powerful ***good*** news of the gospel,[8] You promise that I'm not destined for wrath on Your judgment day, but I'm destined "to obtain salvation through our Lord Jesus Christ, who died for us so that whether we are awake or asleep we might live with him."[9]

Could it be that You're right now giving me a greater intimacy *with* You, Jesus, in my desperate need and longing?

"Oh, how abundant is your goodness, which you have stored up for those who fear you and worked for those who take refuge in you" (Ps. 31:19).

This is so hard, Lord. I feel...

But You promise...

So I trust You with...

Forgive me for...

Please help me...

My song to you is...

Though troubles assail us and dangers affright,
though friends should all fail us and foes all unite,
yet one thing secures us, whatever betide,
the promise assures us, "The Lord will provide."

The birds, without garner or storehouse, are fed;
from them let us learn to trust God for our bread.
His saints what is fitting shall ne'er be denied
so long as 'tis written, "The Lord will provide."

When Satan assails us to stop up our path,
and courage all fails us, we triumph by faith.
He cannot take from us, though oft he has tried,
this heart-cheering promise, "The Lord will provide."

No strength of our own and no goodness we claim;
yet, since we have known of the Savior's great name,
in this our strong tower for safety we hide:
the Lord is our power, "The Lord will provide."

("The Lord Will Provide," Newton, J., 1775)

♪♪♪

God's promise of faithfulness

Father, because You are faithful, I can walk through this trial, even if You choose not to remove it on earth. Your promises hold me when my emotions and thoughts spiral. Suffering can bring such temptation to doubt Your love or to fall into sinful self-pity and bitterness toward You. Suffering zooms "me" into the center of my thoughts. I easily forget You are my faithful and loving Father. But even if I'm faithless, You are faithful.[1] In Your faithfulness that took Jesus all the way to the cross for me, You are "faithful and just" to forgive my sins and purify me from my unrighteousness.[2] Thank You, Lord, that You've given me so many promises of Your faithfulness.

You promise that You won't let me be tempted beyond what I can bear and that You always provide a way out of temptation.[3] Your true Word helps me fight this good fight of faith.[4]

So many of Your promises jump to my heart from Isaiah, written to Your sin-full and beloved, forgiven people.

"Even to your old age I am he; and to gray hairs I will carry you. I have made and I will bear; I will carry and will save" (Is. 46:4).

"He gives power to the faint, and to him who has no might he increases strength" (Is. 40:29).

"For I, the LORD your God, hold your right hand; it is I who say to you, 'Fear not. I am the one who helps you'" (Is. 41:13).

"When you pass through the waters, I will be with you; and through the rivers, they shall not overwhelm you" (Is. 43:2).

In Your promises, I see Your faithfulness. I see that You are the source of my faith, my strength to endure trials. I am not at the center at all. You are.

Jesus, You are the author and perfecter of my faith.[5] Any faith I have, even the tiniest mustard seed-sized bit[6] on the most challenging days, is entirely a gift from You. From beginning to end, Your promised inheritance, Your promised salvation, and Your promised faith rests on Your grace as a guarantee.[7] It's all from You.

So, please help me to hold fast to my gospel hope without wavering. Because, by Your grace, clinging to Your Word and the confession of this hope, You who promised are faithful.[8] As I bring You my pain, as I lament to You with tears and fears, I can sing of Your promise to be faithful to me until the glorious day I see You face to face, seeing eternal and unseen things.

No matter what happens today, help me to sing, "Great is your faithfulness."

This is so hard, Lord. I feel...

But You promise...

So I trust You with...

Forgive me for...

Please help me...

My song to you is...

Here, O my Lord, I see thee face to face;
here would I touch and handle things unseen,
here grasp with firmer hand th'eternal grace,
and all my weariness upon thee lean.

Here would I feed upon the bread of God,
here drink with thee the royal wine of heav'n;
here would I lay aside each earthly load,
here taste afresh the calm of sin forgiv'n.

This is the hour of banquet and of song;
this is the heav'nly table spread for me:
here let me feast, and, feasting, still prolong
the brief, bright hour of fellowship with thee.

I have no help but thine, nor do I need
another arm save thine to lean upon:
it is enough, my Lord, enough indeed;
my strength is in thy might, thy might alone.

Mine is the sin, but thine the righteousness;
mine is the guilt, but thine the cleansing blood;
here is my robe, my refuge, and my peace,
thy blood, thy righteousness, O Lord my God.

("Here, O My Lord, I See Thee Face to Face," Bonar, H., 1855)

♫♫♫

God's promise of gentleness

PRECIOUS LORD JESUS, I'VE READ THAT YOU ARE "GENTLE and lowly in heart."[1] Help me remember the gentle way You treat Your repentant, lowly, suffering ones.[2]

You came into Your created world in a lowly, humbled, and gently meek way. While still fully God, You emptied Yourself as You dependently trusted in our Father, obeying Him all the way to the cross.[3]

In Your gentleness, You promise tender comfort to me in my suffering, for it's also humbling me into a dependent trust of our Father. God, You promise that You are near to my broken heart, saving me as one who is "crushed in spirit."[4] You promise to comfort me when I'm feeling cast down.[5] As I wait for You to bring victorious justice over all sin, evil, and our enemy, You promise you will not break a bruised reed or quench a smoldering wick.[6] Sometimes, my flame seems almost out as I bow so low in need.

But You promise to be my Comforter in those very moments.[7] For they are indeed humbling. I see my need; so do others. Not everyone understands, but You do. I need You...Lord.

Maybe I also need to remember that You are not only gentle, but You are the LORD,[8] my Maker, through Whom and for Whom the heavens and earth exist.[9] It's in Your gentle reminder of Your power and authority to hold up the entire universe, that I am no longer bowed down with an overwhelmed focus on my own dimmed light, but with focus on Your sure promise to hold me up.[10]

"He who is bowed down shall speedily be released; he shall not die and go down to the pit, neither shall his bread be lacking" (Is. 51:14).

It is all Your gentle and tender mercy that this speedy release comes when I am bowed down before Your throne of grace. It's all Your gentle comfort and freeing release when I realize You are the source of all I need to endure this pain today...and tomorrow. I can sing along with David, "You have given me the shield of your salvation, and your right hand supported me, and your gentleness made me great."[11] This very humility is Your gentle and tender gift of saving, rescuing trust in You as You hold me up. Just like You experienced, my gentle Savior. Thank You, for as I take Your yoke upon me and learn from You, You again promise I will find rest for my soul.[12]

"For as we share abundantly in Christ's sufferings, so through Christ we share abundantly in comfort too" (2 Cor. 1:5).

This is so hard, Lord. I feel...

But You promise...

So I trust You with...

Forgive me for...

Please help me...

My song to you is...

Jesus, the very thought of thee
with sweetness fills my breast;
but sweeter far thy face to see,
and in thy presence rest.

No voice can sing, no heart can frame,
nor can the memory find,
a sweeter sound than thy blest name,
O Savior of mankind.

O Hope of every contrite heart,
O Joy of all the meek,
to those who fall, how kind thou art!
How good to those who seek!

But what to those who find? Ah, this
no tongue nor pen can show;
the love of Jesus, what it is
none but his loved ones know.

Jesus, our only joy be thou,
as thou our prize wilt be;
Jesus, be thou our glory now,
and through eternity.

("Jesus, the Very Thought of Thee,"
attr. to St. Bernard of Clairvaux, 12th c., trans. Caswall, E.)

♪♪♪

God's promise of self-control

Holy Spirit, You promise to grow Your self-control fruit in me. I cling to this promise, for I need this freeing truth in all the temptations suffering can bring.

"If the Son sets you free, you *will* be free indeed."[1] What a promise when I forget that my old self was crucified with Jesus and I'm no longer a slave to sinful motivations of my sin nature.[2]

What a promise when I'm tempted to put myself at the center of my life because I'm suffering. When I am tempted to self-pity, self-strength, self-focus, self-preservation, or self-righteousness, You promise to give me all the grace I need for self-control.

With every moment of temptation, please remind me of Your glorious promise:

"But now that you **have been** set free from sin and **have become** slaves of God, the fruit you **get** leads to sanctification and its end, eternal life. For the wages of sin is death, but the free gift of God is eternal life in Christ Jesus our Lord" (Rom. 6:22-23, emphasis added).

You promise self-control as You conform me more and more to the likeness of Jesus, helping me in my weakness, all the way until the day I am glorified.[3] You promise to focus me on Christ's gift of righteousness as my own through faith,[4] Christ's strength as my own,[5] Christ's preserving care into my fears,[6] Christ's comfort in my affliction.[7]

When I'm grasping for control over my suffering, You promise to bring me back to abiding in Your Word as a true disciple of Jesus, because of Your work, indwelling Holy Spirit.[8] I'm just a branch that can't possibly bear fruit unless I remain on the vine, abiding there.[9] Holy Spirit within me, it's all by Your grace and Your promised work to "train" me to live a self-controlled, upright, and godly life right now.[10] A spirit of self-control, power, and love is Your promised gift.[11]

"I have been crucified with Christ. It is no longer I who live, but Christ who lives in me. And the life I now live in the flesh I live by faith in the Son of God, who loved me and gave himself for me" (Gal. 2:20).

"Cast your burden on the LORD, and he **will** sustain you; he will **never** permit the righteous to be moved" (Ps. 55:22, emphasis added).

"And the effect of righteousness **will** be peace, and the result of righteousness, quietness and trust *forever*" (Is. 32:17, emphasis added).

"In returning and rest, you **shall be** saved; in quietness and trust **shall be** your strength" (Is. 30:15, emphasis added).

"O LORD, you hear the desire of the afflicted; you **will** strengthen their heart; you **will** incline your ear" (Ps. 10:17, emphasis added).

"My eyes are awake before the watches of the night, that I may meditate on your promise" (Ps. 119:148).

This is so hard, Lord. I feel...

But You promise...

So I trust You with...

Forgive me for...

Please help me...

My song to you is...

In sweet communion, Lord, with thee
I constantly abide;
my hand thou holdest in thine own
to keep me near thy side.

Thy counsel through my earthly way
shall guide me and control,
and then to glory afterward
thou wilt receive my soul.

Whom have I, Lord, in heaven but thee,
to whom my thoughts aspire?
And, having thee, on earth is naught
that I can yet desire?

Though flesh and heart should faint and fail,
the Lord will ever be
the strength and portion of my heart,
my God eternally.

To live apart from God is death,
'tis good his face to seek;
my refuge is the living God,
his praise I long to speak.

("In Sweet Communion, Lord, with Thee," Psalter based on Psalm 73, p.d.)

♪♪♪

God's promise of wisdom and guidance

GOOD SHEPHERD, THANK YOU FOR GUIDING ME THROUGH this suffering journey. Psalm 23's promises are precious to me, for You are indeed leading me in paths of righteousness, giving me needed moments of rest, restoration, and comfort in Your always-good and compassionate presence. You're leading me, through the darkest places, every single day until I live in the new heaven and earth with You.[1]

Yet I often don't know which way to go or who to believe. It's so confusing. But I turn to You, with reverent awe that You are Lord, and gratitude that I belong to You. I know that fearing and knowing You is the start of my own wisdom and understanding.[2] This suffering journey brings heaps of decisions to make, so I'm clinging to Your promises as I seek Your perfect wisdom.

> "I will instruct you and teach you in the way you should go; I will counsel you with my eye upon you" (Ps. 32:8).

You promise that if I ask my Father, knowing He's always generous to give wisdom,[3] He will give it to me, just as He gave it to You as You walked this earth. He's given me this very faith in You, Lord Jesus! You are wisdom itself, and I'm "in Christ Jesus, who became to us wisdom from God, righteousness and sanctification and redemption."[4]

So, by the work of the Holy Spirit, please illuminate Your Word to me and help me understand it.[5] For You promised that He not only teaches me through it but also brings Scripture to mind when I need help.[6] Savior, please keep me teachable and humble as You were, because Your Word promises: "He leads the humble in what is right, and teaches the humble his way."[7] This affliction is surely humbling me to need Your wisdom, for each moment. Help me trust the guidance of Your Word so I can walk wisely according to Your will, "making the best use of the time" as I suffer.[8]

You promise that it's in that very need, in my lowest, thirstiest, and most desperate places, that You provide this very trust of faith as I meditate on Your Word and rest there. When I'm the driest, when I don't emotionally "feel" Your presence, it's then that I must turn to Your breathed-out Scripture[9] and listen to Your wise teaching with a soft heart to Your tender voice, my Savior and Lord.

> "And the LORD **will** guide you continually and satisfy your desire in scorched places and make your bones strong; and you shall be like a watered garden, like a spring of water, whose waters do not fail" (Is. 58:11, emphasis added).

When I don't know what to do, fill me with wholehearted trust in Your wisdom and not my human understanding, for You promise to make my path straight.[10] Help me to quickly make Your desired course corrections as You lead me by Your Word, out of deep love for You, Lord. Help me cling to Your promised guidance as I rest in how You're specifically applying Your wise and sanctifying teaching to my suffering.

> "'What no eye has seen, nor ear heard, nor the heart of man imagined, what God has prepared for those who love him'— these things God has revealed to us through the Spirit. For the Spirit searches everything, even the depths of God" (1 Cor. 2:9-10).

This is so hard, Lord. I feel...

But You promise...

So I trust You with...

Forgive me for...

Please help me...

My song to you is...

All the way my Savior leads me;
what have I to ask beside?
Can I doubt his tender mercy,
who through life has been my guide?
Heav'nly peace, divinest comfort,
here by faith in him to dwell;
for I know, whate'er befall me,
Jesus doeth all things well;
for I know, whate'er befall me,
Jesus doeth all things well.

All the way my Savior leads me,
cheers each winding path I tread,
gives me grace for ev'ry trial,
feeds me with the living bread.
Though my weary steps may falter,
and my soul a-thirst may be,
gushing from the rock before me,
lo, a spring of joy I see;
gushing from the rock before me,
lo, a spring of joy I see!

All the way my Savior leads me -
O the fullness of his love!
perfect rest to me is promised
in my Father's house above:
when my spirit, clothed, immortal,
wings its flight to realms of day,
this my song through endless ages:
Jesus led me all the way;
this my song through endless ages:
Jesus led me all the way!

("All the Way, My Savior Leads Me," Crosby, F., 1875)

♪♪♪

God promises to provide my needs

~~~~~~

Most High and Almighty God, I'm abiding in Your protecting shelter today, a cooling shadow in this intense heat. You are my refuge in this storm, a fortress in this battle, and I trust You today.[1] Why? Because You are in supreme command over all.[2] Faithful Father, as Your reconciled and saved daughter, I'm safely enfolded under Your loving wings,[3] so I don't need to fear anything that could happen today.[4]

You promise:

> "Because he has his heart set on me, I will **deliver** him;
> I will **protect** him because he knows my name.
> When he calls out to me, I will **answer** him;
> I will **be with** him in trouble.
> I will **rescue** him and **give** him honor" (Ps. 91:14-15 CSB, emphasis added).

As I suffer, I read the verbs in Your precious promises to me, and my heart rests because I do trust in Your name and unchanging character. Thank You that I know You as Lord! Because You're also now my loving Abba Father[5]...and that's how I hold fast to You. I'm held fast in Your love for me in Christ. You've already given me redemption through Christ's blood and the forgiveness of my trespasses. It's all according to the riches of Your grace.[6] Jesus held fast to the cross for me so that I can hold fast to You today.

I also don't need to be afraid of what might happen in the future. You promise to supply everything I need according to Your riches in glory in Christ Jesus,[7] to give me the required strength for whatever lies ahead.[8] Help me to keep seeking, knocking, and asking You for what I need as I pray.[9] But although my immediate thoughts usually gravitate to earthly things, I know what I need most to endure any trial…they're spiritual. This *is* Your always-with-me protecting, delivering, rescuing, honoring, and answering grace, as You promise in Psalm 91, no matter how this trial unfolds in Your loving care for me.

So, help me to hold fast firmly to Your love, seeking first Your righteous kingdom work in my heart, for You promise to add earthly things You know I need too.[10] Help me to hear Your Word, holding it fast in an honest and good heart that You've already planted in me.[11] Give me the soul rest that You promise when I come to Jesus and walk yoked with Him.[12] My heart rests in Your presence and promises, in today's and tomorrow's needs, thrice holy God and my loving Father.

"Though he falls, he will not be overwhelmed, because the LORD supports him with his hand" (Ps. 37:24 CSB).

"He gives strength to the faint and strengthens the powerless. Those who trust in the LORD will renew their strength; they will soar on wings like eagles; they will run and not become weary; they will walk and not faint" (Is. 40:29, 31 CSB).

Jesus says, "I am the bread of life; whoever comes to me shall not hunger, and whoever believes in me shall never thirst" (Jn. 6:35).

This is so hard, Lord. I feel...

But You promise...

So I trust You with...

Forgive me for...

Please help me...

My song to you is...

Be not dismayed whate'er betide,
God will take care of you;
beneath his wings of love abide,
God will take care of you.

God will take care of you,
through ev'ry day, o'er all the way;
he will take care of you,
God will take care of you.

Through days of toil when heart doth fail,
God will take care of you;
when dangers fierce your path assail,
God will take care of you.

All you may need he will provide,
God will take care of you;
trust him and you will be satisfied,
God will take care of you.

No matter what may be the test,
God will take care of you;
lean, weary one, upon his breast,
God will take care of you.

("God Will Take Care of You," Martin, C. D., 1904)

♪♪♪

God promises a forever family of love

ABBA FATHER, YOU MADE A MOST BEAUTIFUL PROMISE TO Your people, offering them hope...six years before Jerusalem and the temple were destroyed. You knew they would need it. Into this very judgment for their sin, You promised: "And I will give them one heart, and a new spirit I will put within them. I will remove the heart of stone from their flesh and give them a heart of flesh, that they may walk in my statutes and keep my rules and obey them. And they shall be my people, and I will be their God...I will put my Spirit within you, and cause you to walk in my statutes and be careful to obey my rules."[1]

Even as Your people continued to forget You, compromising with the sinful ways of this fallen world, You were still unfolding Your promised plan for a forever family of love. Now, all of our sinful thoughts, motivations, words, and deeds were laid on our Savior, Your Son, who bore all the judgment we deserve for sin.

You kept Your promise. Now, the Holy Spirit within us does indeed cause us to want to obey You; this proves to us that we are certainly part of Your family, Your people.[2]

"No one can come to me unless the Father who sent me draws him, and I will raise him up on the last day" (Jn. 6:44 CSB).

"Everyone the Father gives me will come to me, and the one who comes to me I will never cast out" (Jn. 6:37 CSB). For "this is the will of him who sent me: that I should lose none of those he has given me but should raise them up on the last day" (Jn. 6:39 CSB).

"Those who were not my people I will call 'my people,' and her who was not beloved I will call 'beloved'" (Rom. 9:25).

"I will be a father to you, and you shall be sons and daughters to me, says the Lord Almighty" (2 Cor. 6:18).

"The Spirit himself bears witness with our spirit that we are children of God, and if children, then heirs" (Rom. 8:16-17).

"I will not forget you. Behold, I have engraved you on the palms of my hands" (Is. 49:15-16).

I easily forget when suffering makes me *feel* forgotten and alone or when I don't *feel* "beloved." So today, help me remember Your sure and solid promises of the gospel. Along with everyone to whom You've given promised new hearts,[3] help me to remember that "to all who did receive him, who believed in his name, he gave the right to become children of God."[4] God, You are the source of my belonging to Jesus! What a privilege and gift to be in Your family! Help me to remember that You're always my loving Father, and I'm always Your beloved. I can come to You with every thought, seeking Your help when I'm tempted to sin and forget Your amazing grace to me.

No matter how hard things become, nothing can separate me or anyone else in Your true family[5] from Your love.[6] We've all been transferred into Your kingdom of light[7] as citizens of Your heavenly kingdom.[8] In an incredible way, my beloved Jesus is my older brother![9] As I suffer today, but in this intimate fellowship with You, please help me to walk in love[10] with others, especially those in Your forever family.[11]

> "Beloved, we are God's children now, and what we will be has not yet appeared, but we know that when he appears we shall be like [Jesus], because we shall see him as he is. And everyone who thus hopes in him purifies himself as he is pure" (1 Jn. 3:2-3).

> "Your dead shall live; their bodies shall rise. You who dwell in the dust, awake and sing for joy!" (Is. 26:19)

This is so hard, Lord. I feel...

But You promise...

So I trust You with...

Forgive me for...

Please help me...

My song to you is...

Loved with everlasting love,
drawn by grace that love to know,
Spirit sent from Christ above,
thou dost witness it is so.
O this full and precious peace
from his presence all divine;
in a love that cannot cease,
I am his and he is mine.

Heaven above is deeper blue,
earth around is sweeter green,
that which glows in every hue
Christless eyes have never seen.
Birds in song his glories show,
Flowers with richer beauties shine
since I know, as now I know,
I am his and he is mine.

Taste the goodness of the Lord:
welcomed home to his embrace,
all his love, as blood outpoured,
seals the pardon of his grace.
Can I doubt his love for me,
when I trace that love's design?
By the cross of Calvary
I am his and he is mine.

His forever, only his--
who the Lord and me shall part?
Ah, with what a rest of bliss
Christ can fill the loving heart.
Heaven and earth may fade and flee,
firstborn light in gloom decline,
but while God and I shall be,
I am his and he is mine.

("Loved with Everlasting Love," Robinson, W., 1890)

♪♪♪

God promises royal privileges

Abba Father, You are not only the eternal, sovereign, and holy, holy, holy God of all power and might, but You are always my perfectly loving Father.[1] I'm in awe that You've brought me into Your royal family by Your gracious gift of repentance and faith in Jesus Christ as my Lord and Savior.[2] Your tender mercy toward me caused me to be born again to my heavenly inheritance, one for royalty! You promise it's "imperishable, undefiled, and unfading" because You are guarding it by Your power! Even more remarkable, the royal privileges to me are my "living hope" as I suffer because Jesus is resurrected and alive.[3]

By Your abundant grace, You promise that Your royal family members are Your purposefully chosen, adopted "fellow heirs" with Jesus Christ, and we now suffer on earth "with Him."[4] Therefore, I join my royal family in "giving thanks to the Father, who has qualified [us] to share in the inheritance of the saints in light. He has delivered us from the domain of darkness and transferred us to the kingdom of his beloved Son, in whom we have redemption, the forgiveness of sins."[5]

You did this in Your great love for me so I would be "holy and blameless" through my union with Jesus.[6] And somehow, this suffering context is part of it today. But I'm not alone as I suffer. You gave me Your Holy Spirit, the Spirit of Your Son,[7] to inwardly shape me into this "holy and blameless" heir, sealed by Him "for the day of redemption."[8] Seeing Your transforming work in my heart confirms that I am Your heir.[9] Oh Father, thank You!

You give me glorious and comforting details of what lies ahead for me, as I inherit the place You've already made and prepared for me,[10] as a citizen of heaven.[11] Thank You for the beautiful descriptions of what it will be like to see my resurrected and ascended Jesus as He is, to see Your face as Jesus has always seen You, and to live in Your holy and glorious presence forever.[12] Stir my heart into deep gratitude and praise today, for this eternal promise is my sustaining hope...today.[13]

So often, I forget Your promises because I forget who I am as a member of Your royal family. I forget my own identity in Christ. I also forget that You are King over all and Jesus is *my* Lord and King.[14] I easily focus on my earthly suffering or the swirling and escalating darkness around me and forget I'm already transferred into Your kingdom.[15] Please help me remember Your compassion to me as Your beloved child and to be humbly, reverently thankful to You, particularly in the testing of this tempting trial.[16]

I cling to Your promise of blessing to those who remain steadfast when we are "under trial." By Your gracious gift of enduring faith and steadfast love toward me, when I have "stood the test," I "***will receive*** the crown of life, which God ***has promised*** to those who love him."[17] (Jas. 1:12, emphasis added).

This is so hard, Lord. I feel...

But You promise...

So I trust You with...

Forgive me for...

Please help me...

My song to you is...

When I fear my faith will fail,
Christ will hold me fast;
When the tempter would prevail,
He can hold me fast!

I could never keep my hold,
He must hold me fast;
For my love is often cold,
He must hold me fast.

I am precious in His sight,
He will hold me fast;
Those He saves are His delight,
He will hold me fast.

He'll not let my soul be lost,
Christ will hold me fast;
Bought by Him at such a cost,
He will hold me fast.

He will hold me fast,
He will hold me fast;
For my Savior loves me so,
He will hold me fast.

("He Will Hold Me Fast," Habershon, A. R., 1906)

♫♫♫

God promises my righteousness in Christ

HOLY, HOLY, HOLY GOD, YOUR WORD MAKES IT VERY CLEAR that no one can possibly enter into Your presence, because since sin entered our world in Genesis 3, "no one will be justified in [Your] sight by the works of the law...now, apart from the law, the righteousness of God has been revealed...through faith in Jesus Christ to all who believe."[1]

I don't like to think of myself as a sinner, for I like to see myself as a good person, a righteous person even. But Your holy standard isn't possible. Your righteous requirement is always obeying Your law perfectly, always with completely sinless motives. Your holy command is to love You with *all* my heart, mind, and soul and to perfectly love others as myself. Even when I'm suffering.[2]

I do sin, sometimes even turning away from You in my pain. But You tenderly beckon me to re-turn to You, to re-turn to the gospel truth that my righteousness does not come from me and never could; it comes from my righteousness in Christ.[3] It's His perfectly obedient righteousness put into my account, through the faith You've given to me, connecting me to Him.[4] The punishment I deserve for any sin, You have laid on the One who never sinned, in Your covenant love for me as one united with Christ.[5]

As I suffer, help me to cling to this gospel promise when I'm tempted to forget You've already clothed me in Jesus' sinless robe of righteousness. In those moments, I'm then tempted to forget Your compassionate love toward me. I forget what Jesus has done for me on the cross. My heart easily hardens and fears Your judgment, making my suffering even worse as I turn away from Your grace and peace.[6] I start to think I need to pray differently or somehow earn Your love and acceptance to make my pain disappear. I begin to stand on my own works, or how strong or weak I think my faith is, or my wishes for an easy life instead of Christ, the solid Rock.

I see my sin and it's discouraging. But I'm no longer under the law, but under grace in this New Covenant time, so sin no longer rules me![7] Help me to remember and believe Your promised gift, the "righteousness of God that depends on faith" when I'm tempted to think I've done something to earn suffering as punishment for my sins.[8]

Help me to love You and others from a safe and solid place of rest as I look to Jesus' righteousness and "put on the new self" You've already gifted to me, "created after the likeness of God in true righteousness and holiness."[9] For this is why Jesus died in Your deep love for me, to be sin for me.[10] You promise, "By his wounds you have been healed" so I can "die to sin and live to righteousness."[11] Help me to find the happy blessing of those "who hunger and thirst for righteousness"[12] as I continually "practice righteousness" by loving You and others, through Christ who dwells in me by Your Spirit.[13] I'm in Your practice room, continually needing to re-turn to You in this very suffering, but the music will be so sweet!

For You promise my great reward, one wholly of Your grace and gift, from the beginning to that glorious day. "There is laid up for me the crown of righteousness, which the Lord, the righteous judge, will award to me on that Day, and not only to me but also to all who have loved his appearing."[14]

> "The sun of righteousness shall rise with healing in its wings. You shall go out leaping like calves from the stall" (Mal. 4:2).

> [God] "will sustain you to the end, guiltless in the day of our Lord Jesus Christ. God is faithful, by whom you were called into the fellowship of his Son, Jesus Christ our Lord" (1 Cor. 1:8-9).

This is so hard, Lord. I feel...

But You promise...

So I trust You with...

Forgive me for...

Please help me...

My song to you is...

*My hope is built on nothing less
than Jesus' blood and righteousness;
I dare not trust the sweetest frame,
but wholly lean on Jesus' name.*

*On Christ, the solid rock, I stand;
all other ground is sinking sand,
all other ground is sinking sand.*

*When darkness veils his lovely face,
I rest on his unchanging grace;
in ev'ry high and stormy gale,
my anchor holds within the veil.*

*His oath, his covenant, his blood
support me in the whelming flood;
when all around my soul gives way,
he then is all my hope and stay.*

*When he shall come with trumpet sound,
O may I then in him be found,
dressed in his righteousness alone,
faultless to stand before the throne.*

("On Christ the Solid Rock I Stand," Mote, E., 1834)

♪♪♪

I'm completely forgiven! It's God's promise!

Abba Father, because of what Jesus Christ has done for me as my Redeemer and Great High Priest, by Your great grace in the faith You've gifted to me as Your child, I know I'm completely forgiven of all my sin, past/present/future.

But in the throes of pain and suffering, it's so easy to read or hear condemning ideas, and these lies so easily make me afraid of You, as if You were a tyrant, or that my sin or something I've done has brought on this suffering. These are lies of Your enemy, wanting nothing more than for me to turn away from You.

Help me to continually walk in repentance, turning to Jesus and the cross where He bore my sin and shame. Keep me from weakened stewing and fear! Instead, he beckons me to come to Him, learn from Him, take on His easy yoke and Your trusting way of life, and find a freeing rest for my soul.[1] Help me to battle these lies with Your promises!

"There is therefore now no condemnation for those who are in Christ Jesus" (Rom. 8:1).

"I will remember their sins and their lawless deeds no more" (Heb. 10:17).

Help me remember I was once "alienated and hostile in mind, doing evil deeds," but now? I'm totally reconciled to You by Jesus' death.[2] It's all so that You might grow me into Christlikeness, purifying me into holiness before You.[3]

So, all of Your Word's instruction is given to help me "not sin," by making me aware of my sin. But when I do sin, I have an advocate with You, my holy and heavenly Father. He is my only righteousness, Jesus Christ.[4] You purged me with hyssop so I will be clean. You washed me in the blood of the Lamb, promising that I will be whiter than snow.[5]

> "For I will be merciful toward their iniquities and I will remember their sins no more" (Heb. 8:12).

> "But he was pierced for our transgressions; he was crushed for our iniquities" (Is. 53:5).

> "In this is love, not that we have loved God but that he loved us and sent his Son to be the propitiation for our sins" (1 Jn. 4:10).

If I backslide, You promise, "I will heal their apostasy; I will love them freely: for my anger has turned from them."[6] "I myself will be the shepherd of the sheep, and I myself will make them lie down. I will seek the lost, and I will bring back the strayed, and I will bind up the injured, and I will strengthen the weak."[7]

Oh Lord, You are indeed my Good Shepherd! When one of Your sheep wanders off, You go after it![8] When I call to You, You answer me; You're with me in this trouble, and You promise to rescue and honor me[9] all the way home to You.

> "I give them eternal life, and they will never perish, and no one will snatch them out of my hand" (Jn. 10:27).

Hallelujah, it's all You! I'm wholly forgiven, amid this suffering. It's Your promise.

This is so hard, Lord. I feel...

But You promise...

So I trust You with...

Forgive me for...

Please help me...

My song to you is...

*Not what my hands have done
can save my guilty soul;
not what my toiling flesh has borne
can make my spirit whole.
Not what I feel or do
can give me peace with God;
not all my prayers and sighs and tears
can bear my awful load.*

*Thy work alone, O Christ,
can ease this weight of sin;
thy blood alone, O Lamb of God,
can give me peace within.
Thy love to me, O God,
not mine, O Lord, to thee,
can rid me of this dark unrest,
and set my spirit free.*

*Thy grace alone, O God,
to me can pardon speak;
thy pow'r alone, O Son of God,
can this sore bondage break.
No other work, save thine,
no other blood will do;
no strength, save that which is divine,
can bear me safely through.*

*I bless the Christ of God;
I rest on love divine;
and with unfalt'ring lip and heart,
I call this Savior mine.
His cross dispels each doubt;
I bury in his tomb
each thought of unbelief and fear,
each ling'ring shade of gloom.*

*I praise the God of grace;
I trust his truth and might;
he calls me his, I call him mine,*

my God, my joy, my light.
'Tis he who saveth me,
and freely pardon gives;
I love because he loveth me,
I live because he lives.

("Not What These Hands Have Done," Bonar, H., 1864)

♪♪♪

Jesus is praying for me

FATHER, WHAT A COMFORT TO KNOW THAT JESUS IS PRAYING for me as I suffer earthly trials. Along with Your permanent sealing and protection of a true believer by Your indwelling Holy Spirit,[1] this is how I can cling to Your promised and assured end. God, You are the original and continual source.[2] Jesus Himself is the author and perfecter of my faith! He also intercedes for me according to Your perfect will and plan for my life.[3]

So, if I ask anything according to Your will, I can know that You hear me and that I have these requests.[4] Oh Lord, this ongoing suffering is bringing me to pray like my beloved Savior:

"Abba Father, all things are possible for you. Remove this cup from me. Yet not what I will, but what you will" (Mk. 14:36).

I feel the battles daily. In this war with the world,[5] my fleshly desires and the remnants of my sin nature,[6] and Satan,[7] it's simply not my desire to suffer. It hurts, and I'm so wearied in this race of endurance.[8]

But I can rest assured that You're bringing about Your will for my life, all the way home to You. You've given me Your Word as Your answer to my desperate prayers for help, more and more growing me in trusting Your promises, following Your loving instructions to me, and enduring this suffering with persevering faith.

How do I know? Because Jesus promised! And He is praying for me!

"If you love me, you *will* keep my commandments. And I will ask the Father, and he will give you another Helper, to be with you forever, even the Spirit of truth, whom the world cannot receive, because it neither sees him nor knows him. You know him, for **he dwells with you and will be in you**" (Jn. 14:16-17, emphasis added).

"I am praying…for those whom you have given me, for they are yours. I have given them your word, and the world has hated them because they are not of the world, just as I am not of the world. I do not ask you to take them out of the world, but that you keep them from the evil one. Sanctify them in the truth; your word is truth" (Jn. 17:9, 14-15, 17).

In His omniscient understanding of my deepest desires, my emotions, and thoughts, my beloved Jesus is praying for me according to Your will, to sanctify me in the truth of Your Word. I'm so comforted that, before I even come to You in prayer, You promise to answer and hear me[9] and to pour Your water into my thirsty and dry heart by Your Spirit.[10] You promise that all of Jesus' sheep hear His voice, that He knows them and they follow Him.[11] You promise to lead and guide me, and to turn the darkness into light and the rough places into level ground.[12] You promise to help me "be strong and courageous," replacing fear or dismay, because "the LORD your God is with you wherever you go."[13] So, even if this suffering lingers because it's not Your will for it to leave me today, I can cling to Your sure and true promises, as You continue to set me apart from this fallen world.

This is so hard, Lord. I feel...

But You promise...

So I trust You with...

Forgive me for...

Please help me...

My song to you is...

Blessed assurance, Jesus is mine!
O what a foretaste of glory divine!
Heir of salvation, purchase of God,
born of his Spirit, washed in his blood.

Perfect submission, perfect delight,
visions of rapture now burst on my sight;
angels descending, bring from above
echoes of mercy, whispers of love.

Perfect submission, all is at rest;
I in my Savior am happy and blest;
watching and waiting, looking above,
filled with his goodness, lost in his love.

This is my story, this is my song,
praising my Savior all the day long;
this is my story, this is my song,
praising my Savior all the day long.

("Blessed Assurance, Jesus is Mine," Crosby, F., p.d.)

♪♪♪

God is redeeming this suffering

FATHER, WHEN THE HARD DAYS BECOME HARD YEARS OF A hard life, I must remember Your promised redemption, rescue, and deliverance. I continually cherish Your rescuing gift of saving grace. My blessed Redeemer gave Himself for me, cleansing me from sin to purify me for His own possession.[1]

"For I know that my Redeemer lives, and at the last he will stand upon the earth" (Job 19:25)!

You've redeemed and rescued me from my deadness as a sinner,[2] from an empty and futile way of life, one of lawlessness in this world, one that lives for earth's perishing things.[3] Instead, in Your great love for me, You've chosen me to be saved, through Jesus Christ's payment of every debt I owe You as a sinner. Every eternal promise to me as Your beloved child is certain!

So, this earthly suffering must be part of Your redeeming work of sanctifying grace and love toward me...and in me. In Your perfect love for me, You promise that You will sanctify me as Your chosen child, purifying me by the Spirit as I believe in the truth.[4]

This purifying, refining, melting away of my remaining sin nature feels so painful. It's like fire that creates pure gold. Yet, I can see that You're rescuing me to desire sin less and Your righteous ways more and more, because You're gradually giving me new desires.[5] I *need* Jesus more as I suffer, I *love* Him more as I suffer, and I *want* to be conformed more and more to His image.[6] I *want* to love You and others with whatever time You've given me on earth! Oh Lord, I see Your redeeming work! For this suffering is Your gift to help me walk steadfastly,[7] to be zealous for good works.[8] Your strong and tested gift of faith is Your rescuing and delivering grace, a continual and ongoing thing You've promised to do in me as I suffer.

> "Though our outer self is wasting away, our inner self *is **being renewed*** day by day. For this light momentary affliction ***is preparing*** for us an eternal weight of glory beyond all comparison" (2 Cor. 4:16-17, emphasis added).

So, in the hardest moments, when it feels anything but light and momentary, help me cling to Your promised outcome of perfecting work in me. You promise I will receive "praise and glory and honor at the revelation of Jesus Christ,"[9] "that I may obtain the glory of our Lord Jesus Christ."[10] You promise my glorification.[11]

Could this be how I can "count it all joy" today?[12] This joyful end can become my *current* joy when I realize my suffering is Your redeeming work in me, as Your beloved child. As I suffer, I wait for Your promised and blessed hope to see Jesus, perhaps at His return.[13] As I suffer, though I haven't seen him, I do love Him. Though I don't physically see Him right now, I believe in Him. So I can rejoice with inexpressible joy that's filled with glory. Because of Your grace-filled promise, I'm obtaining the outcome of my faith, the salvation of my soul.[14]

This is so hard, Lord. I feel...

But You promise...

So I trust You with...

Forgive me for...

Please help me...

My song to you is...

Redeemed, how I love to proclaim it!
Redeemed by the blood of the Lamb;
redeemed thro' his infinite mercy,
　　his child and forever I am.

Redeemed, and so happy in Jesus,
no language my rapture can tell;
I know that the light of his presence
with me doth continually dwell.

I think of my blessed Redeemer,
I think of him all the day long;
I sing, for I cannot be silent;
his love is the theme of my song.

Redeemed, redeemed,
redeemed by the blood of the Lamb;
redeemed thro' his infinite mercy
his child and forever I am.

("Redeemed, How I Love to Proclaim It!" by Crosby, F., 1882)

♪♪♪

God is transforming me in this suffering

Father, as You sanctify me, this suffering becomes Your transforming work. It's Your ongoing and promised work to me as Your believing child, in Jesus Christ!

"His divine power ***has granted to us all things*** that pertain to life and godliness, through the knowledge of him who called us to his own glory and excellence, by which *he has granted to us*

his precious and very great promises,

so that through them you may become partakers of the divine nature, having escaped from the corruption that is in the world because of sinful desire" (2 Pet. 1:3-4, emphasis added).

What a gift and promise to me as I suffer in this corrupted world of sinful desire. As with all of Your instructions, for example, when You tell me to "be transformed" by the renewal of my mind,[1] You are already making it possible by the transforming work of the Holy Spirit. You are the source of my being "in Christ," from beginning to end![2] I've already been justified, washed, and sanctified in the name of the Lord Jesus Christ, by the Spirit of God.[3]

So, when You tell me to "rejoice always, pray without ceasing, give thanks in all circumstances…do not quench the Spirit," [4] I can know that You will make this possible as I suffer. You promise that You've already given me every spiritual gift I need, united with Christ, "who will sustain you to the end, guiltless in the day of our Lord Jesus Christ. God is faithful."[5] Faithful God, please lead, teach, fill, and guide me, as You promise.

Help me to endure any suffering by clinging to this precious promise of Your sustaining work, with bold confidence in Your continual grace outpoured to me as a member of Your "chosen race, a royal priesthood, a holy nation, a people for [Your] own possession, that [I] may proclaim the excellencies of him who called you out of darkness into his marvelous light."[6] You've given me a new purpose and identity! I'm Your newly created work of art, walking in Your already-prepared good works.[7] You raised Jesus, and You promise to raise me by Your power,[8] continually transforming me into one who is "led by the Spirit."[9] "For all who are led by the Spirit of God are sons of God."[10] In fact, these very battles of suffering and battles with my sin nature are fueling a stronger need for Your indwelling Spirit's help. A desperate one.

You are the ongoing source of all that I need to walk in Your way, Your transforming purpose for the remainder of my earthly life. Oh Father, Jesus *is* the only way to You.[11] I can walk in Your way as I suffer, with rivers of living water within me,[12] by the Holy Spirit's transforming and promised power.

So, I glory in Your magnificent and transcendent name,[13] as the holy God who promises to do a new thing in the midst of this hardship. Who promises to Your people to create a way in the wilderness and to spring up rivers in the desert.[14] His name is Jesus.

> "'For the mountains may depart and the hills be removed, but my steadfast love shall not depart from you, and my covenant of peace shall not be removed,' says the LORD, who has compassion on you" (Is. 54:10).

This is so hard, Lord. I feel...

But You promise...

So I trust You with...

Forgive me for...

Please help me...

My song to you is...

A wonderful Savior is Jesus my Lord,
a wonderful Savior to me;
he hideth my soul in the cleft of the rock,
where rivers of pleasure I see.

He hideth my soul in the cleft of the rock
that shadows a dry, thirsty land;
he hideth my life in the depths of his love,
and covers me there with his hand.

A wonderful Savior is Jesus my Lord,
he taketh my burden away;
he holdeth me up, and I shall not be moved,
he giveth me strength as my day.

With numberless blessings each moment he crowns,
and filled with a fullness divine,
I sing in my rapture, O glory to God
for such a Redeemer as mine!

When clothed in his brightness, transported I rise
to meet him in clouds of the sky,
his perfect salvation, his wonderful love,
I'll shout with the millions on high.

("A Wonderful Savior is Jesus, my Lord," Crosby, F., 1890)

♪♪♪

God is conforming me to the image of Jesus

Father, Your promises all center around Jesus, don't they? Jesus is not only the center of Your glorious love story, but also the center of Your love story for me personally. It was because You loved me so much that You gave Your only Son.[1] "See what kind of love the Father has given to us, that we should be called children of God; and so we are."[2] So somehow, this suffering I'm living through on earth must be part of Your love story, as Your beloved child. For You saved me and called me to a holy calling. It wasn't because of my own works, but because of Your grace and Your own purpose.[3]

Father, what is that purpose for me as one who loves You and is called according to Your purpose? Remind me daily! It's to bear Your family resemblance, to conform me to the image of Your Son, my older brother.[4] It's that I "may know him and the power of his resurrection, and may share in his sufferings, becoming like him in his death, that by any means possible I may attain the resurrection from the dead."[5]

I am becoming more like Jesus, sharing in only a micro-molecule of his sufferings. He suffered in every possible way, all for me, and I'm now united with Him. My old sin nature was nailed to the cross with Him so I'm no longer in bondage to sin. You've set me free from sin's power over me, and death no longer reigns over my life; now Your grace does![6] You've made me alive together with my Lord, Christ Jesus![7]

You promise that, now that I've "been set free" from being enslaved to sin (Rom. 6:7) and instead enslaved to You as one whom the Son has set free, I will be free indeed (Jn. 8:36)! You promise life, peace, and the ability to put the deeds of my remaining sin nature to death, all by the power of Your indwelling Holy Spirit who leads me (Rom. 8:6, 11, 14).

Jesus endured all suffering without any trace of sin. Oh, Father, I constantly sin in thought, word, and deed. Suffering is a tough temptation to sin, especially in my thoughts toward You and others. I bring it all to the cross once again today because You've already "forgiven us all our trespasses, by canceling the record of debt that stood against us with its legal demands. This [You] set aside, nailing it to the cross."[8]

I want to be conformed to the image of Jesus, my beautiful Savior. Through Your Spirit's work within me, by the gospel, Your power "for salvation to everyone who believes," You are now daily helping me live by faith, "from faith for faith."[9] You're bringing about living into the new identity, new creation, new self, new heart You've given to me. On the hard days.

Because yes, this suffering is indeed part of Your gloriously promised purpose for me to become more like Jesus. "Suffering produces endurance, and endurance produces character, and character produces hope, and hope does not put us to shame, because God's love has been poured out into hearts through the Holy Spirit who has been given to us."[10] This suffering is Your loving context for giving me an enduring, hope-filled, "rejoice in our sufferings" kind of faith. In Your perfect love for me, You're deepening my love for the suffering and victorious Lord Jesus, as You prove that I truly belong to Him. This is victory! For it's in the midst of the worst suffering that "we are more than conquerors through him who loved us."[11] Your promises are sure...and You are making it possible, through this suffering.

"To the one who conquers, I will grant to eat of the tree of life, which is in the paradise of God" (Rev. 2:7).

This is so hard, Lord. I feel...

But You promise...

So I trust You with...

Forgive me for...

Please help me...

My song to you is...

Jesus! what a Friend for sinners!
Jesus! lover of my soul;
friends may fail me, foes assail me,
he, my Savior, makes me whole.

Jesus! what a strength in weakness!
Let me hide myself in him;
tempted, tried, and sometimes failing,
he, my strength, my vict'ry wins.

Jesus! what a help in sorrow!
While the billows o'er me roll,
even when my heart is breaking,
he, my comfort, helps my soul.

Jesus! what a guide and keeper!
While the tempest still is high,
storms about me, night o'ertakes me,
he, my pilot, hears my cry.

Jesus! I do now receive him,
more than all in him I find;
he hath granted me forgiveness,
I am his, and he is mine.

Hallelujah! what a Savior!
Hallelujah, what a Friend!
Saving, helping, keeping, loving,
he is with me to the end.

("Jesus, What a Friend of Sinners," Chapman, J. W., 1910)

♫♫♫

God is giving me endurance and strength as I suffer

Holy God and loving Father, this is one of Your most lavish promises to me as I suffer:

"Fear not, for I am with you; be not dismayed, for I am your God; I will strengthen you, I will help you, I will uphold you with my righteous right hand" (Is. 41:10).

When Jesus tells us He came so that we might have abundant life,[1] I realize that Your promise to strengthen me spiritually *is* this life! By Your upholding and indwelling Holy Spirit, it *is* more than I could ever ask for or imagine.[2] You're always with me because I'm in Christ,[3] a sheep who's intimately known by Jesus, who rests in the care of my Good Shepherd,[4] who's already been given the treasure of Your saving and glorious work of Jesus on my behalf. You've already shone Your light into my former life of darkness, showing me Your glory as I see Jesus.[5]

So today, by Your ongoing grace, I can cling to Your promises to hold me up with enduring and strong faith within this trial.

"Even though I walk through the valley of the shadow of death, I will fear no evil, for you are with me; your rod and your staff, they comfort me" (Ps. 23:4).

"God is our refuge and strength, a very present help in trouble" (Ps. 46:1).

Even when I fall, You promise to hold me up, as You direct and establish my steps.[6] Because I'm so needy and dependent on You right now, I can cling to Your promises of abundant grace, gifting me with Your power to walk through this suffering while giving to others as You call me to.[7]

"Now we have this treasure in clay jars, so that this extraordinary power may be from God and not from us. We are afflicted in every way but not crushed; we are perplexed but not in despair; we are persecuted but not abandoned; we are struck down but not destroyed. We always carry the death of Jesus in our body, so that the life of Jesus may also be displayed in our body" (2 Cor. 4:7-10 CSB).

Because I feel so weak and weary, barely hanging on, this abundant life is in Your sustaining me and carrying me by Your continually sanctifying and powerful presence with me. You promise to bring me home to see and live with You forever in Your radiant glory and company. What a gift and treasure, Lord.

It's Your might,[8] giving me endurance and steadfast faith.[9] For this? I can indeed position this trial as all joy, label it as all joy, and view it as all joy, with great hope in Your promised strength of faith.[10]

"He who calls you is faithful; ***he will surely do it***" (2 Thess. 5:23, emphasis added).

"Blessed are those whose strength is in you, in whose heart are the highways of Zion. As they go through the Valley of Baca [a dry, lifeless, weeping valley], they name it a place of springs…They go from strength to strength; each one appears before God in Zion" (Ps. 84:5-7).

Jesus promises to "the one who conquers, I will grant him to sit with me on my throne, as I also conquered and sat down with my Father on his throne" (Rev. 3:21).

This is so hard, Lord. I feel...

But You promise...

So I trust You with...

Forgive me for...

Please help me...

My song to you is...

How firm a foundation, you saints of the Lord,
is laid for your faith in his excellent Word!
What more can he say than to you he has said,
to you who for refuge to Jesus have fled?

"Fear not, I am with you, O be not dismayed;
for I am your God, and will still give you aid;
I'll strengthen you, help you, and cause you to stand,
upheld by my righteous, omnipotent hand."

"When through the deep waters I call you to go,
the rivers of sorrow shall not overflow;
for I will be with you, your troubles to bless,
and sanctify to you your deepest distress."

"When through fiery trials your pathway shall lie,
my grace, all-sufficient, shall be your supply;
the flame shall not hurt you; I only design
your dross to consume and your gold to refine."

"E'en down to old age all my people shall prove
my sovereign, eternal, unchangeable love;
and when hoary hairs shall their temples adorn,
like lambs they shall still in my bosom be borne."

"The soul that on Jesus has leaned for repose,
I will not, I will not desert to his foes;
that soul, though all hell should endeavor to shake,
I'll never, no never, no never forsake."

("How Firm a Foundation," K., 1787)

♪♪♪

God is giving me sufficient grace as I suffer

FATHER, YOU PROMISE, "MY GRACE IS SUFFICIENT FOR YOU, for my power is made perfect in weakness."[1] This suffering has removed so much of my self-sufficiency, my ability to do what I once could. It's made me needy and weary. But Your grace is sufficient because it's in this very experience that I see...I can keep going only by Your power. One hour at a time, You give me sufficient grace in the depths of my soul, my emotions, my heart cries, and my spiritually tired places.

"For I will satisfy the weary soul, and every languishing soul I will replenish" (Jer. 31:25).

"Call upon me in the day of trouble; I will deliver you, and you shall glorify me" (Ps. 50:15).

You're giving me grace for the spiritual battles that are so strong in suffering, by Your indwelling Spirit who is greater than Satan and any of his minions.[2] You're giving me grace when I realize my idolatries, grumbling about things that threaten my comfort and ease, gripping into control rather than releasing to Your care. You give me grace when I'm discontent or impatient. You are so gracious when anything other than the likeness of Jesus Christ in me...isn't shown.

In Your steadfast and covenant love, You called me by Your grace[3] and made me right with You when I received Your "abundance of grace and the free gift of righteousness."[4] What a gift, because I could never live without sinning against Your law's standard of complete perfection. I was born with a sin nature—it's simply impossible on earth. But Jesus perfectly kept Your law so that "the promise by faith in Jesus Christ might be given to those who believe."[5] "A person is not justified by works of the law but through faith in Jesus Christ."[6]

Your gospel of grace tells me that I no longer need to earn Your love or add anything to what You've already done for me in Jesus' finished work on the cross for me.[7] I am Your child now. It's not about me; it's about You now. If I were to trust in my obedience or good works, rather than Christ's righteousness, I would actually be falling away from Your grace.[8]

So, today, help me to trust in Your promises instead, "to the praise of Your glorious grace."[9] For You loved me and gave me *eternal comfort* and *good hope* through grace.[10] You're the One *strengthening* me by this same grace.[11] It's "from [Christ's] fullness we have all received, grace upon grace...grace and truth came through Jesus Christ."[12] You also continually give more grace "to the humble" while You oppose "the proud." [13]

Ah, could this also be part of Your sufficient grace to me, as I suffer? Like Paul, who lived with a nagging thorn to keep him humble,[14] could my humbled need for You in suffering be Your gift of ongoing, sanctifying grace? Could You be helping me humble myself under Your mighty hand, casting my every anxious, upset, controlling, and self-focused concern on You...because You care for me?[15]

> "Because of the truth that abides in us and **will be** with us forever: Grace, mercy, and peace **will be** with us, from God the Father and from Jesus Christ the Father's Son, in truth and love" (2 Jn. 2-3, emphasis added).

This is so hard, Lord. I feel...

But You promise...

So I trust You with...

Forgive me for...

Please help me...

My song to you is...

Rock of Ages, cleft for me,
let me hide myself in thee;
let the water and the blood,
from thy riven side which flowed,
be of sin the double cure,
cleanse me from its guilt and pow'r.

Not the labors of my hands
can fulfill thy law's demands;
could my zeal no respite know,
could my tears forever flow,
all for sin could not atone;
thou must save, and thou alone.

Nothing in my hand I bring,
simply to thy cross I cling;
naked, come to thee for dress;
helpless, look to thee for grace;
foul, I to the Fountain fly;
wash me, Savior, or I die.

While I draw this fleeting breath,
when mine eyelids close in death,
when I soar to worlds unknown,
see thee on thy judgment throne,
Rock of Ages, cleft for me,
let me hide myself in thee.

("Rock of Ages, Cleft for Me," Toplady, E., 1776)

♪♪♪

God keeps His promises, for His glory...my best life!

FATHER, "THIS IS MY COMFORT IN MY AFFLICTION, THAT your promise gives me life."[1]

You promise to give me my best life of grace-filled blessing as I fellowship with my glorious Lord and Savior during this time of suffering. For You have placed me into union with Christ now![2] It's for Your glory, not mine. "For my own sake, I do it. My glory I will not give to another."[3]

This is such an abundant life![4] I'm living with and in my beloved Jesus, now and forever saved from Your rightful condemnation for sin.[5]

"The LORD preserves all who love him, but all the wicked he will destroy."[6]

"God shows his love for us in that while we were still sinners, Christ died for us. Since, therefore, we have now been justified by his blood, much more **shall we be saved** by him from the wrath of God" (Rom. 5:9, emphasis added).

So, Your promise gives me abundant life now. It's by being part of Your glorious love story. Jesus is the central character; I get to be in His story! It's one filled with every spiritual blessing, all Your gift of grace to me, fulfilling Your plan of adopting me into Your family. What gifts of redemption, forgiveness, lavished grace, an eternal glorious inheritance, all sealed by the Holy Spirit.[7]

Every bit of my earthly Christian walk, especially in this challenging time of suffering, is enabled by Your Spirit's work within me. "If you abide in my word, you are truly my disciples, and you *will* know the truth and the truth *will* set you free."[8] "The Spirit of truth...*will* guide you into all the truth."[9] "You know him, for he dwells with you and *will* be in you."[10]

I can trust Jesus' promise that "if anyone loves me, he *will* keep my word, and my Father *will* love him, and we [Father, Son, Holy Spirit] *will* come to him and make our home *with* him."[11] So, as I'm being perfected by Your Spirit, I can rest in all of Your promises to me as Your beloved child. I can know that Your Spirit is praying for me according to Your will, knowing every inward groan as I suffer.[12] I can trust that You'll help me endure this tribulation with courage, contentment, satisfaction, rest, peace, freedom, and safety in Your arms of salvation's refuge, no matter what. I can trust Your living and active Word's[13] direction and course-correction because You are walking with me and guiding me.

"The LORD is my shepherd; I shall not want. He makes me lie down in green pastures. He leads me beside still waters. He restores my soul. He leads me in paths of righteousness for his name's sake" (Ps. 23:1-3).

I can rest in all Your promises to protect me from the evil one because Jesus gave himself for my sin to deliver and rescue me from the present evil age, according to Your will, all for Your glory.[14]

"Submit yourselves therefore to God. Resist the devil and he *will* flee from you. Draw near to God, and he *will* draw near to you" (Jas. 4:7-8, emphasis added).

"Resist him, firm in the faith, knowing that the same kinds of suffering are being experienced by your fellow believers throughout the world" (1 Pet. 5:9 CSB).

"The Lord is faithful. He *will* establish you and guard you against the evil one" (2 Thess. 3:3).

Faithful Lord, You've promised me so much hope as I suffer, so I draw near to You and hold fast to the gospel, Your love story in which You've placed me. I'm living my best and most abundant life right now because I'm living "by the strength that God supplies—in order that in everything God may be glorified through Jesus Christ."[15]

This is so hard, Lord. I feel...

But You promise...

So I trust You with...

Forgive me for...

Please help me...

My song to you is...

Jesus lives, and so shall I.
Death! thy sting is gone forever!
He who deigned for me to die,
lives, the bands of death to sever.
He shall raise me from the dust:
Jesus is my hope and trust.

Jesus lives and reigns supreme;
and, his kingdom still remaining,
I shall also be with him,
ever living, ever reigning.
God has promised; be it must:
Jesus is my hope and trust.

Jesus lives, and by his grace,
vict'ry o'er my passions giving,
I will cleanse my heart and ways,
ever to his glory living.
Me he raises from the dust:
Jesus is my hope and trust.

Jesus lives! I know full well
naught from him my heart can sever,
life nor death nor pow'rs of hell,
joy nor grief, henceforth forever.
None of all his saints is lost:
Jesus is my hope and trust.

Jesus lives, and death is now
but my entrance into glory.
Courage, then, my soul, for thou
hast a crown of life before thee;
thou shalt find thy hopes were just:
Jesus is the Christian's trust.

("Jesus Lives and So Shall I," Gellert, C. F., 1757)

♪♪♪

God promises to help me praise Him

LORD, I WANT TO ADORE YOU, CELEBRATE YOU, THANK YOU, extol You, commend You, honor You, praise You. For You are worthy of praise.[1] On the hardest and saddest days, my emotions are not happy, dancing around, cheery praise. You know this; You designed our brains and bodies that way. But You promise to help me "fear" or honor and revere You, regardless of my circumstances and emotions.

"I will make with them an everlasting covenant, that I will not turn away from doing good to them. And I **will put** the fear of me in their hearts, that they may not turn from me" (Jer. 32:40, emphasis added).

By the person and work of Jesus Christ for me[2] and the Holy Spirit in me, it's Your promised gift to "cause righteousness and praise," a healing gladness in my sadness, a "garment of praise" to replace my "faint spirit," so that You are glorified.[3]

It feels more like a "sacrifice of praise" on the most challenging days,[4] feeling "sorrowful, yet *always* rejoicing."[5]

Ah, maybe that word "always" in Your promises...is Your help for me to praise You today.

Jesus says, "I am with you always, to the end of the age" (Mt. 28:20).

"For David says concerning [Jesus], 'I saw the Lord always before me, for he is at my right hand that I may not be shaken'" (Acts 2:25).

I'm "always carrying in the body the death of Jesus" so that Jesus' life is shown in my own body (2 Cor. 4:10).

Jesus "is able to save to the uttermost those who draw near to God through him, since he always lives to make intercession for them" (Heb. 7:25).

"Then we who are alive, who are left, will be caught up together with them in the clouds to meet the Lord in the air, and so we will always be with the Lord" (1 Thess. 4:17).

Maybe Jesus' promises of "all" heighten my praise even more!

"With man this is impossible, but with God all things are possible" (Mt. 19:26).

"All authority in heaven and on earth has been given to me" (Mt. 18:18).

"All things have been handed over to me by my Father, and no one knows who the Son is except the Father, or who the Father is except the Son and anyone to whom the Son chooses to reveal him" (Lk. 10:22).

"For the Father judges no one, but has given all judgment to the Son" (Jn. 5:22).

"I have said all these things to you to keep you from falling away" (Jn. 16:1).

By Your grace, with Your help, maybe I can "rejoice in the LORD *always!*"[6] Maybe it comes from trusting Your promises to me, in and through my Lord and Savior, Jesus Christ. Help me, Lord.

This is so hard, Lord. I feel...

But You promise...

So I trust You with...

Forgive me for...

Please help me...

My song to you is...

Rejoice, the Lord is King:
your Lord and King adore!
Rejoice, give thanks, and sing,
and triumph evermore.

Jesus the Savior reigns,
the God of truth and love;
when he had purged our stains,
he took his seat above.

His kingdom cannot fail,
he rules o'er earth and heav'n;
the keys of death and hell
are to our Jesus giv'n.

He sits at God's right hand
'til all his foes submit,
and bow to his command,
and fall beneath his feet.

Rejoice in glorious hope!
Our Lord, the Judge, shall come,
and take his servants up
to their eternal home.

Lift up your heart, lift up your voice!
Rejoice, again I say, rejoice!

("Rejoice! The Lord is King!" by C. Wesley, 1744)

♪♪♪

God promises my suffering will end

HOLY, HOLY, HOLY GOD, I LONG FOR ALL SUFFERING TO END on earth, yet I know this has been a decaying, fallen-into-sin cursed, and groaning world,[1] since Genesis 3. Therefore, when I ache for my own earthly suffering to end, I need to remember that I'm longing for the last chapter of Your love story, when all suffering will end in a new heaven and earth.[2] As Your beloved in Christ, You promise my suffering will ultimately end when You restore and renew everything.

In that beautiful ending scene, where You dwell with Your people redeemed by the blood of Jesus Christ, I will hear You say, "Behold, I am making all things new."[3] It's something I'll never see in this current fallen world, for this is still something unseen.[4] So, I wait with sure hope!

I wait for Your promised execution of perfect justice for sin and complete eradication of evil and Satan when Jesus returns to judge.[5] For You promise that You will punish the world; in other words, those who refused You, the wicked, those who remain lost in their inborn sin, rather than being clothed in Christ's righteousness.[6] I read Matthew 24, Joel, Amos, Ezekiel, Obadiah, Haggai, Daniel, or Revelation and I shudder at the horror that will come upon them on the last day.

And yet, I'm only comforted by knowing this has to happen as You bring Your glorious love story for Your people to its last page of history, as promised and already written. "The grass withers, the flower fades, but the word of our God will stand forever" (Is. 40:8).

"And he will swallow up on this mountain the covering that is cast over all peoples, the veil that is spread over all nations. He will swallow up death forever; and the Lord GOD will wipe away tears from all faces, and the reproach of his people he will take away from all the earth, for the LORD has spoken" (Is. 25:7-8).

My weeping may last throughout every day and night on this earth, but Your joy will come to me in the everlasting morning of Your love story.[7]

Father, I'm overwhelmed and humbled that I now live in Your eternal love story as one whose name is written in "the Lamb's book of life,"[8] one who has the name of Jesus on my forehead,[9] sealed by the Holy Spirit for "the day of redemption,"[10] saved from the promised and necessary wrath that will come for sin. You promise my suffering will end because of this last chapter and page, in which You remove all sin.

"Let not your hearts be troubled. Believe in God; believe also in me. In my Father's house are many rooms. If it were not so, would I have told you that I go to prepare a place for you? And if I go and prepare a place for you, I will come again and will take you to myself, that where I am you may be also" (Jn. 14:2-3).

"The Lord will rescue me from every evil deed and bring me safely into his heavenly kingdom. To him be the glory forever and ever. Amen" (1 Tim. 4:18).

"And the ransomed of the LORD shall return and come to Zion with singing; everlasting joy shall be upon their heads; they shall obtain gladness and joy, and sorrow and sighing shall flee away" (Is. 51:11).

"And this is the promise that he made to us—eternal life" (1 Jn. 2:25).

"He will wipe away every tear from their eyes, and death shall be no more, neither shall there be mourning, nor crying, nor pain anymore, for the former things have passed away" (Rev. 21:4).

"For I consider that the sufferings of this present time are not worth comparing with the glory that is to be revealed to us" (Rom. 8:18).

This is so hard, Lord. I feel...

But You promise...

So I trust You with...

Forgive me for...

Please help me...

My song to you is...

Joy to the world! The Lord is come:
let earth receive her King;
let ev'ry heart prepare him room,
and heav'n and nature sing,
and heav'n and nature sing,
and heav'n, and heav'n and nature sing.

Joy to the earth! The Savior reigns:
let men their songs employ;
while fields and floods, rocks, hills, and plains
repeat the sounding joy,
repeat the sounding joy,
repeat, repeat the sounding joy.

No more let sins and sorrows grow,
nor thorns infest the ground;
he comes to make his blessings flow
far as the curse is found,
far as the curse is found,
far as, far as the curse is found.

He rules the world with truth and grace,
and makes the nations prove
the glories of his righteousness
and wonders of his love,
and wonders of his love,
and wonders, wonders of his love.

("Joy to the World," Watts, I., 1719)

♪♪♪

God promises His glorious restoration, my hope

FATHER, SON, AND HOLY SPIRIT, I'M CLINGING TO YOUR promises as I suffer in this fallen world. Promises help me see my sure future, as I wait for the rest of Your forever family to come to repentance.[1] It is sure because Your glorious love story ends with Your glorious restoration of all things, my eternal hope. Help me to daily re-see this ending with "full assurance...through faith and patience," as one who will inherit Your promises.[2]

> "For you have died, and your life is hidden with Christ in God. When Christ who is your life appears, then you also will appear with him in glory" (Col. 3:3-4).

Yes, the current heavens and earth will be destroyed, but Your "salvation will be forever."[3] In my resurrected body,[4] I will live with You forever, by Your great grace in giving me Christ who is my life. Your glorious love story, written for Your people, Your forever family, will fulfill every promise...forever.

> "My dwelling place shall be with them, and I will be their God, and they shall be my people" (Ezek. 37:27).

> "I will make my dwelling among you, and my soul shall not abhor you.

And I will walk among you and will be your God, and you shall be my people" (Lev. 26:11-12).

"Behold, the dwelling place of God is with man. He will dwell with them, and they will be his people, and God himself will be with them as their God" (Rev. 21:3).

"For the promise is for you and for your children and for all who are far off, everyone whom the Lord our God calls to himself" (Acts 2:39).

"The redeemed shall walk there, and the ransomed of the LORD shall return and come to Zion with singing; everlasting joy shall be upon their heads; they shall obtain gladness and joy, and sorrow and sighing shall flee away" (Is. 35:18-19).

"No longer will there be anything accursed, but the throne of God and of the Lamb will be in it, and his servants will worship him" (Rev. 22:3).

I again remember that You promise this "light and momentary affliction" prepares me for this very glory, with the glorious and holy King.[5] This glory is unseen, eternal, and can't be compared to anything else I've experienced.[6]

So I cling to Your promises with hope as I suffer today. For, in the span of eternal time and unseen reality, my suffering is truly light and momentary. You carry me now, and You will carry me into Your arms, forever. Please, let me see Your glory as I walk through this valley, with You, Lord.[7]

"'Surely, I am coming soon.' Amen. Come, Lord Jesus!" (Rev. 22:20).

"Now to him who is able to keep you from stumbling and to present you blameless before the presence of his glory with great joy, to the only God, our Savior, through Jesus Christ our Lord, be glory, majesty, dominion, and authority, before all time and now and forever. Amen" (Jude 24).

"Now may the God of peace who brought again from the dead our Lord Jesus, the great shepherd of the sheep, by the blood of the eternal covenant, equip you with everything good that you may do his will, working in us that which is pleasing in his sight, through Jesus Christ, to whom be glory forever and ever. Amen" (Heb. 13:20-21).

This is so hard, Lord. I feel...

But You promise...

So I trust You with...

Forgive me for...

Please help me...

My song to you is...

'Tis so sweet to trust in Jesus,
just to take him at his word;
just to rest upon his promise;
just to know, "Thus saith the Lord."

O how sweet to trust in Jesus,
just to trust his cleansing blood;
just in simple faith to plunge me
'neath the healing, cleansing flood!

Yes, 'tis sweet to trust in Jesus,
just from sin and self to cease;
just from Jesus simply taking
life and rest, and joy and peace.

Jesus, Jesus, how I trust him!
How I've proved him o'er and o'er!
Jesus, Jesus, precious Jesus!
O for grace to trust him more!

I'm so glad I learned to trust thee,
precious Jesus, Savior, Friend;
and I know that thou art with me,
wilt be with me to the end.

('Tis So Sweet to Trust in Jesus," Stead, L. M. R., 1882)

♪♪♪

Glory be to the Father
and to the Son and to the Holy Ghost,
as it was in the beginning,
is now, and ever shall be,
world without end. Amen, amen.

("Gloria Patri," anon., 2nd century)

♪♪♪

Notes

INTRODUCTION

1. 1 Corinthians 16:13

1. GOD IS A PROMISE-KEEPER

1. Genesis 12:1-3
2. Genesis 13:14-15
3. Genesis 15:5
4. Genesis 15:6
5. Genesis 16
6. Genesis 17:1
7. Genesis 17:7
8. Genesis 22:8
9. Genesis 22:17-18
10. Romans 4:20-22
11. Galatians 3:9
12. Galatians 3:16. 29
13. e.g., Leviticus 26:12; Numbers 23:19; 2 Samuel 7:28; 1 Kings 8:23; Song of Solomon 6:3; Micah 5:2; Zechariah 4:9-10
14. Romans 4:23-25; Ephesians 1
15. John 8:58

2. PROMISES OF A FAITHFUL GOD

1. Deuteronomy 30:15-18
2. Galatians 3:10
3. Deuteronomy 30:6
4. Deuteronomy 30:20
5. Deuteronomy 31:16
6. Joshua 1:5; Hebrews 13:5
7. Isaiah 7:14; Matthew 1:21-23
8. Matthew 5:17-20
9. Romans 3:10, 12
10. Philippians 2:8
11. Hebrews 9:12
12. Ephesians 1:3-4

3. GOD'S AMAZING "NEW COVENANT" PROMISES!

1. Jeremiah 31:31-34; Ezekiel 16:60; Luke 22:20; 1 Corinthians 11:25; Hebrews 13:20-21
2. Romans 1:1-6
3. 2 Corinthians 3:6
4. Hebrews 8:13

5. Ezekiel 36:26; Galatians 2:20
6. 2 Corinthians 5:17
7. 2 Corinthians 1:20

4. AMAZING GRACE, HOW SWEET THE SOUND

1. John 3:16-17, 10:26-27; Hebrews 9:12, 15; 1 Peter 1:3-5; 1 John 2:25, 5:11-12
2. Romans 3:21-28, 4:3-8; Ephesians 1:7-12; Colossians 2:13-15; Titus 3:4-7
3. Romans 8:28-39
4. Revelation 21:5
5. 1 John 3:2
6. Ecclesiastes 3:11; Isaiah 65:17; Habakkuk 2:14
7. Colossians 1:13
8. Hebrews 9:28
9. Acts 4:12
10. Acts 26:17-18

5. OUR PROMISED LAND

1. Joshua 3
2. Jeremiah 23:5-6; Romans 4:22-25, 8:10, 10:4, 9-11; 1 Corinthians 1:30; Ephesians 4:24; 1 John 2:28-29
3. Colossians 3:1
4. Ephesians 2:6
5. Philippians 3:21
6. John 14:2-3
7. Hebrews 9:15
8. Isaiah 25:6
9. Revelation 19:6-9
10. Isaiah 11:6-9
11. 1 Corinthians 15:19; 2 Corinthians 4:18; Colossians 1:5
12. Psalm 23:6
13. Psalm 19:1
14. John 1:14
15. James 1:17

6. GOD PROMISES HIS ABIDING PRESENCE AND FRUIT

1. Exodus 40:34-38; Deuteronomy 31:6-8
2. Acts 2:17-21
3. John 7:38-39a
4. Mark 14:24
5. John 14:26
6. 1 Corinthians 6:19-20; 2 Corinthians 1:21-22
7. 2 Corinthians 5:5; Galatians 4:6-7
8. Philippians 2:12-13
9. Ezekiel 36:27
10. John 17:17; 2 Thessalonians 2:13-14
11. Galatians 5:16
12. Romans 8:26-27
13. John 15:26

14. Proverbs 1:13; Romans 8:14
15. 1 John 4:4
16. James 3:18
17. Philippians 1:11

7. GOD'S PROMISE OF PEACE

1. Isaiah 9:6
2. Romans 5:1
3. Ephesians 2:13-16; Colossians 1:20
4. Ephesians 6:15
5. Luke 2:14
6. John 16:33
7. 2 Thessalonians 3:16, emphasis added
8. Philippians 4:4-9
9. 2 Corinthians 12:10; Philippians 4:11-13
10. Philippians 4:19
11. John 14:27; Galatians 5:22; Philippians 4:7
12. Romans 8:6
13. John 14:26
14. Philippians 4:4-7; Colossians 3:15-16
15. Isaiah 26:3
16. Isaiah 26:12
17. 2 Peter 3:14

8. GOD'S PROMISE OF LOVE

1. 1 John 4:8
2. Romans 3:26, 5:8-9; 1 John 4:9-10
3. 1 John 4:19
4. John 3:16
5. 1 Chronicles 16:34
6. 1 John 4:18
7. 1 Thessalonians 5:8-9
8. Psalm 143:8
9. Ephesians 3:18
10. Ephesians 3:17
11. Deuteronomy 6:4-5; Joshua 22:5; Mark 12:30
12. 1 John 3:23
13. John 17:26
14. Ephesians 1:6
15. Leviticus 19:18; Matthew 22:39

9. GOD'S PROMISE OF JOY

1. John 15:11, 17:13
2. John 14:16; Galatians 5:22, 25
3. Philippians 4:4; 1 Thessalonians 5:16
4. Acts 26:18
5. Jude 1:24
6. Romans 5:11
7. Colossians 1:11

8. Psalm 51:12
9. Romans 15:13
10. Hebrews 12:2

10. GOD'S PROMISE OF PATIENCE

1. Romans 8:23
2. e.g., Psalm 86:15; 1 Peter 3:9
3. Exodus 34:6
4. 1 Thessalonians 5:9
5. Colossians 1:11
6. Psalm 40:1
7. Romans 8:23-25; 2 Corinthians 4:16-18; Hebrews 11:1
8. Philippians 3:20
9. 2 Peter 3:9
10. Titus 2:13; James 5:7-8
11. Colossians 3:12
12. Psalm 37:7
13. Romans 8:29
14. 1 Timothy 1:16
15. Psalm 62:1
16. Psalm 130:5

11. GOD'S PROMISE OF KINDNESS

1. Romans 2:4
2. Hosea 11:4
3. Matthew 11:29
4. Matthew 11:28
5. Ephesians 2:7
6. Psalm 145:17
7. 2 Corinthians 6:4-5
8. Galatians 5:25
9. Ephesians 4:32
10. Proverbs 31:26
11. Ephesians 1:13
12. Philippians 2:13

12. GOD'S PROMISE OF GOODNESS

1. Romans 8:28
2. Genesis 50:20
3. Psalm 34:8
4. James 1:17
5. Matthew 7:7-11
6. John 10:11
7. 1 Timothy 6:12
8. Romans 1:16-17
9. 1 Thessalonians 5:9-10

13. GOD'S PROMISE OF FAITHFULNESS

1. 2 Timothy 2:13
2. 1 John 1:9
3. 1 Corinthians 10:13
4. 1 Timothy 6:12
5. Hebrews 12:2
6. Luke 17:6
7. Romans 4:16
8. Hebrews 10:23

14. GOD'S PROMISE OF GENTLENESS

1. Matthew 11:29
2. Isaiah 57:15
3. Philippians 2:8
4. Psalm 34:18
5. 2 Corinthians 7:6
6. Isaiah 42:3; Matthew 12:20
7. Isaiah 51:12
8. Amos 5:8
9. Isaiah 51:3; 1 Corinthians 8:6; Colossians 1:16; Hebrews 1:2
10. Psalm 63:8, 145:14; Isaiah 9:7, 41:10; Hebrews 1:3
11. Psalm 18:35
12. Matthew 11:29

15. GOD'S PROMISE OF SELF-CONTROL

1. John 8:36, emphasis added
2. Romans 6:6
3. Romans 8:26-30
4. Philippians 3:9
5. Ephesians 3:16
6. 1 Peter 5:7; 1 John 4:18
7. 2 Corinthians 1:4
8. John 8:31; 1 John 4:13
9. John 15:4
10. Titus 2:12
11. 1 Timothy 1:7

16. GOD'S PROMISE OF WISDOM AND GUIDANCE

1. Psalm 23
2. Proverbs 9:10
3. James 1:5-7
4. 1 Corinthians 1:30
5. 2 Timothy 2:7
6. John 14:25-26.
7. Psalm 25:9
8. Ephesians 5:15

9. 2 Timothy 3:16
10. Proverbs 3:5-6

17. GOD PROMISES TO PROVIDE MY NEEDS

1. Psalm 91:1-2
2. Psalm 91:3, 6, 10-13
3. Psalm 91:4, 16
4. Psalm 91:5-6
5. Galatians 4:7
6. Ephesians 1:7
7. Philippians 4:19
8. Deuteronomy 33:25
9. Matthew 7:7-8
10. Matthew 6:33
11. Luke 8:15
12. Matthew 11:28-30

18. GOD PROMISES A FOREVER FAMILY OF LOVE

1. Ezekiel 11:19-20, 36:26
2. Hebrews 10:15-16
3. Ezekiel 36:26
4. John 1:12
5. Ephesians 5:25-27
6. Matthew 16:18; Romans 8:38-39
7. Colossians 1:13
8. Philippians 3:20
9. Hebrews 2:11-12
10. Ephesians 5:1-2
11. John 13:34-35; 1 John 1:6

19. GOD PROMISES ROYAL PRIVILEGES

1. 1 Chronicles 29:11; Psalm 93:2; Isaiah 46:10; Jeremiah 32:17; Mark 14:36; Galatians 4:6; 1 John 4:18
2. Mark 1:15; Romans 10:9-10; Ephesians 2:8-9; 2 Peter 1:3, 10-11
3. 1 Peter 1:3-5
4. Romans 8:14-17
5. Colossians 1:12-14
6. Ephesians 1:4-5
7. Romans 8:9
8. Ephesians 4:30
9. Galatians 4:6-7
10. John 14:2-3
11. Philippians 3:20
12. Revelation 1:12-18, 21:22-27, 22:3-5
13. Romans 5:2, 8:24-25; 2 Corinthians 4:18
14. Psalm 47:8, 93:1; Daniel 7:13-14; John 18:36; Hebrews 1:3-4; Revelation 17:14, 19:13, 16
15. Psalm 145:13; Daniel 7:27; Matthew 25:34; Colossians 1:12-13

16. Matthew 18:4; Hebrews 12:28
17. James 1:12

20. GOD PROMISES MY RIGHTEOUSNESS IN CHRIST

1. Romans 3:20-22
2. Matthew 22:37-39
3. 1 Corinthians 1:30
4. Romans 3:21-22, 4:6-11, 24-25, 10:4
5. 2 Corinthians 5:21
6. Romans 5:1; Galatians 1:6, 8
7. Romans 6:14
8. Galatians 5:5; Philippians 3:9
9. Ephesians 4:24
10. 2 Corinthians 5:21
11. 1 Peter 2:24
12. Matthew 5:6
13. 1 John 3:9-10
14. 2 Timothy 4:8

21. I'M COMPLETELY FORGIVEN! IT'S GOD'S PROMISE!

1. Matthew 11:28-29
2. Colossians 1:21-22
3. Romans 8:29; Titus 2:14; Hebrews 9:14; 1 John 3:3
4. 1 John 2:1
5. Psalm 51:7
6. Hosea 14:4
7. Ezekiel 34:15-16
8. Luke 15:1-7
9. Psalm 91:15

22. JESUS IS PRAYING FOR ME

1. Ephesians 1:13-14, 4:30
2. Hebrews 12:2
3. Romans 8:26-27, 33-34
4. John 14:14; 1 John 5:13-14
5. John 15:19; Revelation 17:4
6. Romans 8:7; Galatians 5:17
7. Ephesians 6:12; 1 Peter 5:8
8. Hebrews 12:1
9. Isaiah 65:24
10. Isaiah 44:3; John 4:14
11. John 10:27
12. Isaiah 42:16
13. Joshua 1:9

23. GOD IS REDEEMING THIS SUFFERING

1. Titus 2:14
2. Ephesians 2:1
3. 1 Peter 1:18-19
4. 2 Thessalonians 2:13
5. Philippians 2:12-13
6. Romans 8:29
7. James 1:2-4
8. Titus 2:14
9. 1 Peter 1:7
10. 2 Thessalonians 2:14
11. Romans 8:16-17, 30
12. James 1:4
13. Titus 2:12
14. 1 Peter 1:8-9

24. GOD IS TRANSFORMING ME IN THIS SUFFERING

1. Romans 12:2
2. 1 Corinthians 1:30; 2 Corinthians 3:16
3. 1 Corinthians 6:11
4. 1 Thessalonians 5:16-19
5. 1 Corinthians 1:8-9
6. 1 Peter 2:9
7. Ephesians 2:10
8. 1 Corinthians 6:14
9. Galatians 5:18
10. Romans 8:14
11. John 14:6
12. John 14:4
13. Psalm 105:3
14. Isaiah 43:19

25. GOD IS CONFORMING ME TO THE IMAGE OF JESUS

1. John 3:16
2. 1 John 3:1
3. 2 Timothy 1:9
4. Romans 8:29
5. Philippians 3:10
6. Romans 6:5-11, 14
7. Colossians 2:13
8. Colossians 2:14
9. Romans 1:16-17
10. Romans 5:3-4
11. Romans 8:37

26. GOD IS GIVING ME ENDURANCE AND STRENGTH AS I SUFFER

1. John 10:10
2. Ephesians 3:20-21
3. Galatians 3:26
4. John 10:14
5. 2 Corinthians 4:6
6. Psalm 37:23-24
7. 2 Corinthians 9:8
8. Ephesians 6:10
9. Revelation 13:10
10. James 1:2-4

27. GOD IS GIVING ME SUFFICIENT GRACE AS I SUFFER

1. 2 Corinthians 12:9
2. 1 John 4:4
3. Galatians 1:15
4. Romans 5:17
5. Galatians 3:22
6. Galatians 2:15
7. John 19:30
8. Galatians 5:4
9. Ephesians 1:6
10. 2 Thessalonians 2:16
11. 2 Timothy 2:1
12. John 1:16-17
13. James 4:6; 1 Peter 5:5
14. 2 Corinthians 12:1-10
15. 1 Peter 5:6-7

28. GOD KEEPS HIS PROMISES, FOR HIS GLORY...MY BEST LIFE!

1. Psalm 119:50
2. 1 Corinthians 1:30
3. Isaiah 48:11
4. Philippians 4:12-13
5. Romans 8:1
6. Psalm 145:20
7. Ephesians 1
8. John 8:21-22
9. John 16:13
10. John 14:17
11. John 14:23
12. Romans 8:22, 27
13. Hebrews 4:12
14. Galatians 1:3-5
15. 1 Peter 4:11

29. GOD PROMISES TO HELP ME PRAISE HIM

1. Psalm 18:3
2. 1 John 2:2
3. Isaiah 61:3, 11
4. Hebrews 13:15
5. 2 Corinthians 6:10, emphasis added
6. Philippians 4:4

30. GOD PROMISES MY SUFFERING WILL END

1. Romans 8:22
2. Isaiah 65:17-25, 66:12-14, 22-24; Revelation 21, 22
3. Revelation 21:5
4. 2 Corinthians 4:18
5. Zechariah 14:4-5,9; Revelation 14, 19-20
6. Isaiah 13:11; Luke 19:10; John 3:3; Acts 3:19-21; Romans 6:23; 1 Corinthians 1:18-32
7. Isaiah 30:5
8. Revelation 21:6
9. Revelation 22:4
10. 2 Corinthians 1:22; Ephesians 1:13-14, 4:30

31. GOD PROMISES HIS GLORIOUS RESTORATION, MY HOPE

1. 1 Peter 3:9
2. Hebrews 6:11-12
3. Isaiah 51:6
4. 1 Corinthians 15
5. Psalm 2:6, 15:1, 24:3, 48:1, 99:9; Isaiah 65:25; Zechariah 8; Revelation 21:10
6. 2 Corinthians 4:17-18
7. Exodus 33:18

About Lauri Hogle

Lauri A. Hogle, PhD, music therapist, music educator, and church musician, heads Singing Christ's Hope, a nonprofit ministry found at laurihogle.com. Her words and musical offerings have touched lives across the globe. Lauri's prayer journal books, including _Near to God_ and _Singing the Gospel to Job_ are complemented by weekly playlist gifts for suffering Christian women. Her lifelong passion is to glorify God through music, teaching, research, and writing. By God's grace in healing, her greatest joy is as wife, mother, and Nana.

Also by Lauri A. Hogle

Near to God: A Devotional Bible Study of God's Character in Our Suffering

Some comments from readers:

"Such an amazing book to help in healing."

"My heart always wanders to focus on self, especially in the midst of fiery trials. What a treasure to have a tool like this that plucks me out of the ash heap of my own misery and sets me on high places, worshipping my great God!"

"Such an encouraging book—true comfort and hope"

"The author points to Scriptures that will engage your heart and mind; and will lead you into fruitful times of worshipping in spirit and truth, finding true comfort and being able to exult in His mercies, His love, and our true hope."

"The devotionals are God-focused instead of focused on looking inward."

"This devotional book is a close friend to any who are suffering."

"A simple devotional length with rich treasures to find each day. Wrapping each day up with songs of worship."

"A must-have."

Singing the Gospel to Job: Finding Hope in Suffering

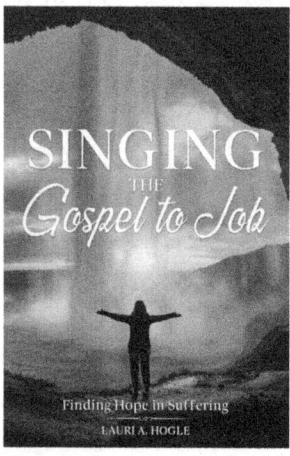

Some comments from readers:

"A **must-read** for those who are going through extended suffering or counsel or care for those who are suffering."

"If you or someone you know walks the path of suffering, take up this book as a kind gift of **gospel rest and hope.**"

"This book and the Scriptures highlighted spoke to my hurting heart. She did a beautiful job explaining simply really tough theological concepts. As she guided, I soaked in."

"This book has been one of the best resources I have found as I walk through deep suffering. It brings me straight to the Word of God and fills me with Truth that comforts, convicts, and sustains me."

"It is beautifully written and is one of the very few books of its kind that I can actually relate to."

"Lauri Hogle's book ministered to my soul as she applied a robust understanding of God's sovereignty in difficult providences to the practical struggles of life. Lauri does an excellent job communicating the hard truths of the book of Job, and how God uses His people's suffering for their good and His glory. Her personal story helps make difficult truth simple to understand and will be a balm for the souls of weary sufferers."

"If you are suffering today, in this book you'll find an author familiar with some of the deep questions of your heart and mind, and someone who constantly points you back to the Good News of Jesus Christ and the truth of His Word."

"Lauri, with raw honesty, tackles the painful questions that arise in our hearts when suffering is our constant companion. By massaging the truth of God's Word into our hearts, she brings us to Jesus."

"Born from her own circumstances, Lauri Hogle uses the narrative of Job to point Christians to the only true hope we have when we suffer in life—the living Word of God. Then, in each chapter, she challenges us to sing those truths to ourselves through classic hymns of the Christian faith."

Made in United States
North Haven, CT
02 March 2024